T
AU
STORIES
2005

THE BEST AUSTRALIAN STORIES 2005

Edited by
FRANK MOORHOUSE

Black Inc.

Published by Black Inc.,
an imprint of Schwartz Publishing Pty Ltd

Level 5, 289 Flinders Lane
Melbourne Victoria 3000 Australia
email: enquiries@blackincbooks.com
http://www.blackincbooks.com

ISBN 1 86395 110 5

Contents

Memorandum from the Editor

Frank Moorhouse

Most readers would intelligently construe the term 'best', as in the title *Best Australian Stories* as an aspiration, but not a term to be taken papally. It is also historical. *Best Australian Stories* is modelled on the American *Best Short Stories* series begun as *Best Short Stories of 1915* and, in various reincarnations, still going (and which I collect).

But nor would I argue that the selection is simply subjective, as is sometimes said. Yes, I take only stories that entertain my intelligence and that I appreciate. But my judgement is also formed by having written and read stories for years, having edited other anthologies, and having thought about the short story form. Finally, there is always some discussion of the stories with friends and associates such as Tim Herbert, Xavier Hennekinne, Joanna Logue and Nadine Davidoff. I am gratified when those writers whom I have selected who have never before been published receive attention from my colleagues.

I do not choose with the idea of meeting a range of tastes or trying to, say, represent all Australian states, or all genres of the form. Last year I sought stories from throughout Australia and received about a thousand stories from some six hundred writers. But this year I was unable to commit this amount of time to the task; I think it is now beyond a single editor to read all stories that are out there.

So this year *Best Australian Stories* firstly called for submissions from the membership of the Australian Society of Authors – three thousand members – and from other writers, groups, and from writers who'd been published in earlier editions of *Best Australian Stories.* I then looked to the literary magazines – including the *Griffith Review, Southerly, Westerly, Meanjin, Overland, Island* and *Heat* for stories and I considered stories that had come in for *The Monthly,* a new publication owned by the company that publishes *Best Australian Stories,* and which is publishing a story each month.

I was a judge of the $10,000 Josephine Ulrick national short story competition – the most lucrative of the competitions – and selected stories from the four hundred entries to that competition. I attended a few literary festivals and listened to writers read their work and picked up some stories there as well – I found the stories from Tara June Winch and Karen Manton at the Northern Territory Literary Festival. And finally, some stories just came in and I read those. Adding it all up, I still read about five hundred stories from which I chose twenty-five.

I am pleased that there are both well-known names and new names in the book – Patrick Cullen, Melissa Goode, Alison Ravenscroft and Tara June Winch are published here for the first time. I had no hesitation in breaking with *Best Australian Stories* practice and selecting Patrick's triptych of stories for inclusion. I am especially pleased to have again been offered fine stories from the youngest writers of last year's anthology – Alli Barnard, eighteen, and Nathan Besser, twenty-five – both of whom seem to be continuing as emerging storytellers, and by the way, a couple of the contributors are in their late sixties. The order of stories in the book this year is alphabetical.

In reply to some criticism, none of the writers in *Best Australian Stories 2004* were there just because of promise (nor, conversely, were they excluded or included because of reputation). They were there because they had told a fine story in Australia in the year 2004, a story which I preferred to all the others I read. The same principle applies to this year's anthology.

One of the dangers of competitions and selections for an anthology is that you find yourself taking the best of those offered rather than stories which are distinguished when judged against the wider world of story-writing. I have tried to assess each story against the wider world of writing – as a good story well told – and not to take just the best on offer. I do not see *Best Australian Stories* as having the role of encouraging new or young talent, although I suppose the very existence of the anthology is an encouragement to new talent in an otherwise discouraging environment for the short story. But in my selection of the stories, young and new talent has to win its way against all the stories that come in.

Some of you may be aware that last year's *Best Australian Stories* attracted unusual media attention and I wrote to the *Sydney Morning Herald* saying that it was a long time since a short story anthology had been controversial. For those interested in the short story form, I direct their attention to a few pieces I wrote following publication of *Best Australian Stories 2004*: 'Secrets of the Confessional' (*Bulletin,* 18 January 2005), an analysis of the content of the stories which came in for selection; another for the 'Review' (*Weekend Australian* 21–26 December 2004) on the future of the short story as a form; and a piece for 'Spectrum' (*Sydney Morning Herald,* 16–20 February 2005) where I compared *Best Australian Stories 2004* with *Best American Stories 2004.* The *Bookseller and Publisher,* March 2005, reported my survey of the contributors to *Best Australian Stories 2004.* The survey looked at age, training, education, place of residence, aspirations, religion and so on. I compared it to a similar survey I did in 1984 when I edited a short story anthology for Penguin, *State of the Art.*

Although I believe romantically that fiction writing is a personal and solitary art, I do have to accept that there are other pathways to creativity and from biographical notes and resumes that accompanied many of the stories, I found a few patterns. (By the way, resumes and biographical notes, while of great interest to me as an observer of the practices of writing, are irrelevant in my selection of stories.)

These included the proliferation of prizes run by local and regional government and the spread of writing groups either formally organised as workshops and classes or self-organising informal groups. Many of the smaller prizes use the lottery-form of funding, that is, entrants pay a fee which provides the prize money.

One of the 'group' ways of becoming a writer came to my attention through the accompanying biographical notes. It is also in some ways a tribute to a teacher of writing, Janey Runci, who has a story in this volume as do two of her former students, Amra Pajalic and Sue Robertson.

Amra and Sue were tutored by Janey at the Centre for Adult Education in Melbourne. Sue Robertson says her love of writing was fostered and continues to be nurtured by a group spawned by Janey and the Victorian Centre for Adult Education, known as the Tuesday Writers; it has has been running for five years.

Sue says, 'The numbers at Tuesday workshops vary from between six and twelve, at least half of whom have been with us since the beginning.

'Janey's influence? Whoa – wouldn't know how to start. When I began with her in 1998 I already had stories published in the *Australian Women's Weekly* when Jenny Rowe was the editor, and had taken out the Chinese Egg Cup Award in a Carmel Bird workshop for the best short story in a group with her, but I'd had a few "bad" years and had fallen by the writing wayside ...

'Janey's passion for writing and for teaching writing was infectious ... And her style of workshopping is one we have taken with us into Tuesday Writers.'

Amra says, 'I did Janey's class as part of my Diploma of Arts and Professional Writing and Editing at the Council of Adult Education. Janey did a great mix of writing exercises and practical information about how to get published ... This was also the year that made me believe I was a writer ... They say that when you examine your life there are a handful of people who have most inspired you, and Janey is definitely one of them.'

Janey Ranci began her career when she graduated with honours in English from the University of Melbourne and then took a diploma in education. Janey wrote to me as follows, 'In summary, I've taught adults for most of my working life, beginning in the neighbourhood centre world, giving support classes to adults who were returning to study. I began seriously writing, sending out and getting published myself in 1989, had some success and received a Writers Project Grant from the Australia Council.'

Janey is obviously an inspiring teacher and we know that much teaching of writing is happening in Australia at present.

My survery of the writers accepted for *Best Australian Stories 2004* revealed that fifteen of the twenty-five writers had completed a writing course. Of these, three said it was of no value and one said the course had been of qualified value. One said it had been harmful and another said it had only been a way to meet other writers. I suppose the question has to ultimately be asked: what happens to the students' writing if the teacher is harmful or misleading? (Among the contributors were two high school dropouts.)

The *Australia Council Report on the Arts Economy* 2003 found that writers nominating 'self-taught' or 'learning on job' as the most important part of their development accounted for 52 per cent of the writers surveyed.

The answer, I suppose, is that there are many paths to becoming a writer.

Frank Moorhouse, 2005

How to Love Broken Glass

Alli Barnard

I'm going.

Yeah? Why? He slammed shut the fridge and skulked into the lounge room.

I'm destroying you.

This world's destroying me, you're only part of it.

So do you want me to stay, or leave? He didn't turn around so I said it to his back.

Do what you want. He flopped onto the couch and stared at nothing. Or maybe he just stared at anything that wasn't me.

It is nearly dark now. The streetlights should be on. They aren't.

Then I'm staying.

And that is how it became a test of endurance.
We'd rather kill each other than be the first to leave.

When I first met him, in all my glowing ignorance, he'd said he was an agnostic.

An agnostic?

It's like an atheist with commitment issues.

Do you have commitment issues?

It was a joke. Gemma's friend, right?

Kate. Wanna drink?

Not gonna ask who I am?

Figured you'd tell me if you wanted me ta know.

It was his first smile all night. If vampires smile they would smile like that.

Then there were the parties; the pre-people nausea followed by the post-booze nausea and all the sickness in between. I would be too busy laughing with my friends to notice he was too busy laughing with his.

At least that's what we pretended.

He'd ignore me all night and then we'd drunkenly fuck before the tweekers had gone home.

Mark said you were a bastard and that he would never treat me like that. I almost believed him till he tried to grope me in the kitchen *You're so special Kate* beer breath slurring, face so close I could see every sweaty black pore.

I ran to find you and you held me. Told whoever it was flirting with you to *fuck off* and held me.

He is just a beautiful ghost.

Moods are contagious, personalities are contagious, everything's contagious. If I stay here maybe I'll catch a fatal case of malignant arsehole and then where will we be? Rotting together with last week's dishes.

But there is always one more last straw.

I walk past him on his smugly embracing couch, junkie vomit-coloured daffodils. The eyes don't even flicker. I am jealous of the furniture, this is infinitely sad. I hope a meteorite crashes through the roof and there is nothing left of the perky fabric but a burning hole in the carpet.

He wanted it to hurt and I would let him. One of us might as well be happy. It was always less fuss to give in.

Do you think you could love me? Am I here so you don't have to? Has this ever ever made you happy?

I had started a list of things I would never say.

We used to fight, loud and desperately.

You coward!

Fuck you, you fuckin' worthless fuckin' princess.

Get out.

No.

Get out!

Make me.

The violent sex that always followed felt like we were still attacking each other. There was a volatile sort of passion there; I don't think we care enough to fight anymore.

The next day I would wake up in bruises, flinching through crowded hallways. The scratches in his skin left blood on the sheets. He was always gone when I got up. I felt him leave but pretended not to. Maybe he knew I was awake, but he never let on.

Carefully I washed the sheets and hung them, clingy and translucent, in the small patch of sun in the garden. He would be out when I got home at night and I would go to bed and pretend I didn't notice he wasn't there. Clumsy and drunk he'd blunder in through the darkness and kiss the back of my neck and I'd pretend I hadn't been lying there for hours waiting for him, wondering where he was – *figured you'd tell me if you wanted me to know.*

He slept touching my back; I slept on the very edge of the mattress. When he stirred with the daylight he would wrap himself around me until it seemed that every part of him was touching every part of me, and his breathing said he was asleep again. I would be awake before this, lying dead still. Half in sleep and foggy we lay together. I would try to match my breathing to his.

Maybe it was so it would seem like we belonged together,
maybe it was so he would think so.
But he probably never noticed anyway.

Every few months we'd do it again, our routine; put off shut off blast off. Then we'd spend weeks getting high.

Lying here watching the music explode around my head, feeling parts of my body race to be the first to go dead; I was dreaming of tortured wastelands circled by hundreds of crumbling satellites, metal corpses drifting though space and nothing but dust to remember who made them.

And doesn't broccoli look like little trees?
And why do blue veins bleed red? And why am I ... ?

Kate Katekatekate –

What?

You know your name rhymes with cat? And and you know what else? You have a pussy.

Shut up – I can't hear the music.

Pass the Tim Tams.

They miss his head, crash, scatter on the floor and are still, like petrified roaches.

Fuck! What the fuck? Is this a period thing?

Nope.

Good ... His hand slides up my jeans and under the waistband like a parasite.

Get off me.

Talking to him stoned was like that feeling you get running in cold weather with too many layers on, like having hot jelly poured down your back except on the wrong side of the skin.

Last winter he punched me and my lip split.

He scooped me up

and I apologised for bleeding on his shirt.

Lucia or I Can't Really Describe the Sensation

Nathan Besser

I can't really describe the sensation but if it looked like anything, it would look like the surging, upward dome of a firework. The freesailing sparkles flying skyward, pushing through the night. It's like I could fill the sky with that same energy. It probably doesn't make sense to you. It barely makes sense to me.

I can feel when it is coming, and it often has to do with girls. Especially with girls that I'll never be able to kiss. You know those sorts of girls? The ones whose necks are lily-white like silk, and when they turn their heads to laugh at a joke or look at a passing bird you can see their tendons and blue veins pulsating away, and you can see it because their skin is soft, smooth and transparent. Those girls whose hair hangs in a curly black bob that coils behind their ears and without knowing it, they'll push a stray length of hair away from their eyes. When they do that with a smile on their face, or any look of simple joy, I can feel it coming. Of course it never happens. I don't actually burst, but that's what it feels like. And Lucia is one such girl who does that to me.

*

I never really had much luck with girls and that's why I started seeing prostitutes. The first time I was about twenty years old. I was drunk and alone in a bar, and had been rejected by a girl with short black hair and bright red lipstick. The details don't really matter, everyone knows the feeling. The humiliation of a half-decent girl politely telling you to fuck off. It's a universal emotion, like when you're grounded by your father and you cry and cry and then the pain just passes with time. There are some children who keep on arguing and tell their dad to get lost and cop a beating or get grounded. And though I wasn't one of those children, I guess I'm one of those adults. At least that's what I thought I was doing when I staggered towards a brothel looking to pay a woman for sex. I was standing up for myself, taking my power back.

It was a horrible experience by any stretch of the measure. It didn't take me long to realise that the last thing I'd get from a prostitute was a feeling of power. I chose a girl called 'Candy' because there was a darkness in her eyes, a thinly veiled vulnerability. People always like what's familiar, and if there's anything familiar to me, it's vulnerability. We went into a plain room with folded towels and a floral bedspread.

'What's your real name?' I asked.

'Candy is my real name as far as you're concerned.'

'Sorry. I was just asking. I'm nervous.'

'Are you here to fuck or talk, kid?'

'Both, I guess.'

'It's your money.'

*

After Candy it took me a long while before I had the courage to go back to a brothel. Eventually, I learnt that not all working girls are as impatient and coarse as Candy. Lucia was the opposite of Candy. She'd smile and laugh and be friendly like a regular person. I'd usually spend about half of my allotted hour just chatting and joking with her. She always had these silly jokes to tell me, the sort that you laugh at in primary school. 'Where do fish go for fun … Tuna Park' or 'Where do frogs put their coats … In the croakroom.' I'd try and memorise a few before I went to see her, which was every Thursday night at 6.30 p.m. I worked as a bartender and it cost me a lot of money, but I never regretted it for a moment. It's only money. After about twenty minutes or half an hour we'd eventually have sex. It would happen during a lull in the conversation, or after our laughter started thinning out. By that stage we'd be lying on the bed, and I'd reach my arm over and place it on her stomach. All of a sudden she'd start massaging me and we'd do it. That transition was always difficult, from conversation to sex. Especially when she did it so abruptly. It's like when you are tossing and turning in your sleep with a full bladder, and in a thrust of impatience you rush for the bathroom half-asleep. That was how she had sex with me – just getting it over with. At first I felt bad about it because I liked her so much, but after a while it seemed normal, just like she was my girlfriend and this was the way we did things. I figured the reason why she sometimes rushed it was because she liked talking to me so much.

I spent most of the week looking forward to seeing Lucia. I started having a recurring dream where I'd see her on a street corner, and I'd chase after her but she would always be out of reach. If I did catch up to her, she'd look at me blankly and say, 'Sorry I have to go now' and walk away again. I could never keep up no matter how fast I ran. These dreams exhausted me. When I woke up I felt like I hadn't slept at all. Well, as it turns out, those dreams weren't far from the truth.

*

'Why do you come here?' She once asked me, out of the blue.

'To see you.'

I could tell she was in a weird mood.

'I guess I should tell you that I'm quitting.'

I felt my chest sucked downwards, through the unmade bed.

'Are you going to work somewhere else?'

'No, definitely not.'

I was silent. It was after we had slept together and I was lying on the bed and she was in the shower. We often spoke as she was scrubbing herself in the shower. Washing away the traces of me. She rotated her head around the stream of water so it didn't wet her hair.

'Well, what are you going to do?' I asked.

'I'm not sure. I'll probably get a job as a waitress or something.'

'Oh.'

'I'm telling you this because I like you. I think you're a nice guy.' She paused and looked down, 'I just can't do this work anymore.'

'I understand.'

'Thanks.'

Sure I could understand why Lucia didn't want to be a working girl anymore, but all I could think about was being alone. Being without her.

'Do you think maybe we could see each other for a coffee or something another time?' I asked.

'I'm sorry. But I don't really think so. You see, I'm trying to forget this episode in my life.' She briskly rubbed a towel over her breasts, and then down each leg, 'I'm sorry.'

*

I tried ignoring the feeling. I tried pretending that I wasn't heartbroken, that after all, Lucia was a prostitute. Because to admit that I loved her would be to admit that I was a man whose only intimacy was shared between dollars and sex and floral bedspreads and a girl whose eyes were like a dark icy pool. I still haven't described how she looked. Her shoulders were rounded and her neck rose up to her chin in an undefined slope. Her breasts hung to the sides so her nipples were like antennas and she was knock-kneed. These imperfections were so attractive to me, they were crystals of her purity and vulnerability, and I thought I would be safe. Safe in the transaction of it all.

It's so simple it makes me sick. It's simple because I think of it like a hunter and his prey. I think of the way I spoke and laughed with her so I could encircle her heart before I went in for the kill. It never happened, I never captured her heart. Her eyes captured me and sometimes I wonder if I was the prey and she was indeed the hunter.

I thought I'd never recover. I spent the days before work sitting on my balcony and watching cars speed along Syd Einfeld Drive. Any life or vivacity was slowly leaving me with every hour that went by. I was watching the boat of my life sail away on a clear blue day, slowly dissolving into the horizon until it disappeared.

*

The story almost ends here, but not quite, because I saw Lucia again by chance. I was at the train station and saw her standing with a loose bag slung over one shoulder, and her weight on one leg. She was wearing a short skirt and I never realised her skin was so white, even when she exposed so much of it to me. My heart started thumping and I found it hard to breathe, but I couldn't pass up the opportunity to speak to her. She had earphones in her ears, and I tapped her on the shoulder. She turned around and took out her earphones.

'Hi Lucia.'

She furrowed her eyebrows in confusion.

'Remember me?' I said.

She looked around nervously and then tried to smile but didn't really succeed.

'Yeah. Hi, how are you?'

'I'm OK, I guess. Did you get that job as a waitress?'

'Umm. Well I'm actually working in an office now.'

I looked at her, confused.

'I'm a secretary.'

'I'm glad to hear it Lucia.'

'My name isn't Lucia, it's Kathryn.'

'Oh.'

A train rattled and screeched and filled the empty tunnel like a wave of silver water.

'Anyway, it was nice to see you again.' Lucia said, readjusting her bag.

I looked down at my shoes, trying to think of something to say. I had rehearsed it a million times. It's hard to put emotions and hopes into words, especially when the person hearing them doesn't really care to.

'Umm, Lucia,' I began, 'I just wanted to tell you ...' I looked up and saw that she had already placed her earphones back in her ears and was facing the approaching train as if I didn't exist.

By the time I was out of the station, I remembered what I wanted to tell her. A stupid joke – 'Where does the king keep his armies? ... Up his *sleevies.*' If only I had told her that, then she would have had a coffee with me, or at worst – remembered me forever.

*

I went to see a prostitute only one more time after that. It was in the week when I bumped into Lucia at the train station. The prostitute was from somewhere near Croatia and didn't speak much English. Because we couldn't communicate well, we had sex pretty quickly. I didn't really know what else to do, but I guess that's what I was there for. After we had sex I cried while she was in the shower. She patted me lightly on the shoulder, 'It's OK. Men always crying here.'

I loved Lucia so much, even without knowing her. I loved her because I thought I could inflate her with my energy. But instead of filling her up, I drained myself. Or maybe I wasn't aware that it was working in reverse – Lucia was filling me up with her sadness.

The Other Place

David Campbell

I don't like it when they do that. Pa and Mary.

'Time for jiggy-jiggy,' says Pa, his body filling the doorway. I can smell the whisky.

'Go!' whispers Mary. 'Quickly. It won't take long.'

So I climb out the window and drop to the ground. I run to the barn and pull the old horse blanket over my head to shut out her cries. I squeeze my eyes shut tight and think of the sun falling soft on the yellow leaves as they dip and sway in the late afternoon breeze. It is a living thing, the breeze. It brings life to a dead land, and I follow its path back over the red soil plains to the Mountains of the Moon where our world begins.

At least that's what Mary says. Late at night, when the noises of the house have finally gone, she holds me close and takes me to The Other Place.

'Beyond the Mountains of the Moon it's all green and gold and the people wear clothes that are so white they have special eyeglasses to stop them going blind. Every house has a meadow full of sweet-smelling grass so that the animals have plenty to eat in the morning before they lie down for a rest in the shade of the red gums. The children have a swing and lots of toys and the river is a bright blue pool of water to lie in when it gets too hot. When the sun goes down the whole family gathers while Ma plays the piano and Pa leads the singing. It's the best time of day. And when the music is over, Tom and Mary go to sleep high up in the attic where the cool breeze moves the curtains so the moonlight paints silver patterns on their faces as they sleep.'

Once a week Pa goes into town.

'Be back at dusk. Mind you get them chores done. You hear me, Tom, make sure you get 'em all in the top paddock or I'll tan your hide. Don't want to go losin' any buggers like you did last time.'

It is our day. We get the work done quickly and Mary cuts us some bread and cheese to take down to the big old rock by the creek bed. We sit in the shade of the river red gum, under the scar made by the old people when they cut their canoe, and talk to Ma. Down there, near where the water made the cave in the big flood, is the place we put her. The cross has gone, but there's still a pile of stones.

'We're OK,' says Mary. 'Spite of what he says, he won't whip Tom no more 'cos Tom's too big. He's gettin' old, Ma. He ain't as strong as he used to be and he don't need the jiggy-jiggy so much. Them lumps in his leg won't go away and he limps a lot. He's gonna die soon, I reckon.'

We listen, but there is no sound. The Mountains of the Moon dance in the heat. Sometimes, when there is water, there are pelicans and cormorants. Not today. In the distance old man kangaroo stands dark and solid, his head on one side as if watching. But he cannot see us.

She grins at me. 'You'd be proud of Tom, Ma. He ain't a boy no more. It don't matter if Pa ain't here. Tom's the man now, you hear. Tom's the man.'

'I'm the man, Ma,' I say.

We walk back to the house and into the big bedroom.

'The suit,' says Mary. 'Today you be the suit and I'll be the print dress. The one with the yellow and blue flowers.'

The shirt collar is way too big, but I knot the tie real tight to hold it in. Then I put on the shiny old suit with the buttons missing and the trousers with the cuffs that drag on the ground. The straps on the braces are broken so I use a piece of string for a belt. Mary helps me to lace the shoes.

She spreads the dress on the bed, running her fingers over the faded flowers. It was Ma's Sunday best, but the material is worn and moth-eaten. She strips off her shirt and shorts and I see the bruise, a purple stain just under the swell of her left breast.

'Did he … ?'

She glances down.

'Ain't nothin',' she says. 'I bruise easy, is all. Like I said, he's an old man. Clumsy, too. Now help me with these buttons.'

She stands in front of the cracked mirror, her hands smoothing the thin cotton over her legs. She reaches into the drawer and lifts out the heavy tin box, the holder of Ma's secrets. Her fingers move slowly over the little pots and jars. She chooses one, dips the brush, and traces it gently over her lips until they glow cherry-red in the afternoon light.

'You're beautiful, Mary, just like Ma used to be. Ain't nobody as pretty as you.'

And she smiles, lifting her arms to free the combs from her hair so that the long dark mass falls about her shoulders. She moves her head and I feel an ache in my chest as the shiny black curtain brushes gently across her face.

'It's time, Tom,' she says.

I go outside and wait for a few minutes on the verandah. The breeze has just come in and a small spiral of dust slips across the yard. We have two hours until dusk.

'I'm home, dear,' I say, and open the door to The Other Place.

Mauve

Patrick Cullen

Paul was in the spare room, taking boxes down from the cupboard when Carol came home for lunch. He'd already covered the top of the desk and was putting the last of the boxes on the floor when she came down the hall and stopped in the doorway.

'You're home early,' his wife said.

He looked up and nodded.

'Is something wrong?'

'No, I'm just taking some time off.'

Carol took her bag off her shoulder and lowered it to the floor. She sat at the chair beside the desk. 'How long?' she asked. 'How long are you taking off?'

Paul looked out the window. There was a fig tree out on the footpath; its roots had lifted the bitumen and its branches overshadowed the front of their terrace. 'A week or two,' he said. 'A month, maybe.'

'Why?' she said. 'Why so long, Paul?'

'I need a break.'

'But the kids in Year 12 have their exams. They've almost finished and they'll need you there.'

'They'll get by without me,' he said. He opened a desk drawer, took out some scissors and ran them through the tape on one of the boxes. He folded back the flaps. The box was full of notebooks and loose sheets of paper. He took out some of the paper and looked at the front and back of each sheet.

'What are you looking for?' she asked, leaning toward the opened box.

'I'm not sure,' he said. 'But I'll know when I find it.' He put the paper back into the box and folded the flaps back down. He pulled another box over.

Carol put her hand on top of the box and held it there until Paul looked at her. 'You'll have to go back,' she said. 'You know that you will have to go back.'

'I know,' he nodded and knelt beside the boxes on the floor with the scissors in his hand. 'I'm just going to take a little time off now and then I'm going back to finish the year off.'

'Good,' she said and got up from the chair. 'What are you going to do with yourself until then?'

'I don't know.'

'That's not what I wanted to hear.'

'I'm going to sort out some things. Fix some things,' he said, sliding the scissors beneath a box flap. He looked up at her. 'I'm going to spend some time with you.'

'Good answer,' she said, shaking her head and smiling. 'I'm making lunch if you want something.'

'No,' he said. 'I'm not hungry yet.'

Carol picked up her bag and headed toward the kitchen. 'You will have to go back,' she called as she made her way down the hall, the heels of her shoes striking against the floorboards.

Paul got up off the floor and sat at the desk. He pulled a box toward him. He started reading. There were pieces of paper on which he'd written short phrases or single words. The paper had yellowed, the ink had faded and some of the handwriting was barely legible. He recognised the handwriting as his own but he couldn't feel any of it in the grip of his fingers.

Carol stopped at the spare room on her way back to the library. 'What is all of this anyway?' she asked.

'All sorts of things,' Paul said.

'What will you do with it all after you find what you're looking for?'

He looked at the boxes on the desk and floor. 'Put them back up out of the way, I guess.'

'Why don't you just get rid of them? Do you really think you're ever going to need any of it?'

'Some of it, maybe. But I haven't yet found what I'm looking for.'

'Will you get rid of the rest of it though? When you've found what you're looking for, will you get rid of the rest of it?'

He looked at the boxes on the desk and the floor. The corners of his mouth tightened and he shook his head a little. 'I don't think I can.'

Paul was still sitting at the desk when Carol came home from work. He put the pen down and closed the notebook as she came into the spare room.

'What were you writing?'

'Nothing,' he said. 'I was trying to but I couldn't think of anything to write about.'

'You haven't written anything for such a long time.'

'I know,' he nodded.

'Why not?'

He shrugged his shoulders. 'I don't know,' he said. 'Maybe I've never had anything to write about.'

'What did you used to write?'

'Stories,' he said. 'A few poems, but mostly stories. Bits of stories.'

'Were they any good?'

'I thought so then,' he said. 'But I'm not so sure anymore.'

'Why not?'

'They just don't feel right.'

'Can I read some of them?'

'No, I don't think I want you to.'

'Well, did you find what you're looking for, at least?'

'No,' he shook his head. 'Not yet.'

'How long do you think it will take to find what you're looking for?'

'As long as it takes,' he said. 'The only thing I know for sure is it'll be in the last place I look.'

'Do you know what would be better?'

'What?'

'If you would just give up on that and start fixing some things around here,' she said. 'You could make better use of this time.'

'But I want to do this. I need to do this,' he said.

Carol leaned against the doorjamb and watched him working his way through the boxes. Two of the boxes were back sitting on the floor beside the cupboard and he saw her looking at them.

'It smells stale in here,' she said. 'Open the window. Let in some air.'

He leaned across the desk and undid the latch on the window. He tried to slide up the sash. 'It won't budge,' he said.

'Maybe that's the first thing you can fix,' she said. 'I'm sure there's plenty of other things you can do too.'

'Probably,' he nodded.

'You could start on the bathroom. I don't know how long it is since you said you'd do that. I bought the tiles, remember? They're still out in the shed, aren't they? You should fix up the bathroom, Paul. That's what you should do.'

It was early evening when Paul went out into the courtyard. The sun had set over the suburbs and the starlings were at it in the trees behind the house. The pavers were warm beneath his feet, and they rocked and shifted and pinched his soles as he walked across to the shed.

In the shed he saw that the washing in the machine was ready to come out so he pulled it into the basket and took it out to the clothesline. Carol was sitting on the back step watching him cross the courtyard. She shook her head at him.

'What?' he asked. 'What? It needs to be done.'

'I know,' she said. 'And I always do it. You should just do what you need to do.'

He put the basket down beneath the clothesline and went back into the shed. He looked at the tools that for years he'd said he would use on the house one day. He moved aside the rolled off-cuts of carpet and lengths of timber he thought he would find some use for. He found the tiles and carried them out onto the back verandah. Carol had picked out the tiles when he had first talked about fixing up the bathroom. At the time she'd asked what he thought of the tiles and he had said, 'They'll do the job.'

After the earthquake, when the first of the tiles came away from the wall, Paul had shaken his head and said that they were lucky that he hadn't already redone the bathroom. 'It would've been a waste,' he said. 'To have it all falling down now.'

Carol stood at the washing line while Paul carried the tiles up onto the back verandah. He sat on the back step. 'I'll get started tomorrow,' he said.

'If it wasn't for tomorrow – ' she said.

'I'll start tomorrow,' he said. 'I will.'

They ate dinner in front of the television and after they'd finished Paul took their plates to the sink. Carol went up to bed and Paul went into the spare room. He was still in the spare room when she came back down after midnight. He had a lamp on and was leaning over the desk with his elbows splayed and his head in his hands. She put her hand on his shoulder. He turned quickly. She put her hand up to her chest and twisted a handful of her nightie into her palm. 'I thought you were asleep,' she said.

He leaned back in the chair and stretched.

'No, I'm still at it.'

'I wish you'd come to bed,' Carol said.

'I'd like to,' he said. 'But I need to finish this.'

'Don't forget tomorrow.'

Paul looked at Carol and rubbed at the corner of his eye.

'The bathroom,' Carol said. 'You're starting on the bathroom tomorrow.'

Paul was already at the kitchen table when Carol came down for breakfast. 'I've already seen Ray this morning and he said that we can shower at his place.'

Carol nodded and moved about in the kitchen.

'Kettle's boiled.'

'Thanks,' she said, and took a mug down from the shelf beside the sink. She poured water from the kettle and levered the lid off a tin of coffee. 'I don't remember you coming to bed.'

'I didn't,' Paul said. 'I slept on the lounge.'

'Why?'

'I got tired of sitting at the desk,' Paul said. 'I went into the lounge room to read. I only made it through a couple of things before I fell asleep. It was already light when I woke and I didn't think it was worth going up to bed for only an hour or so.'

Carol nodded and made toast. She sat at the table with her coffee. 'What's your plan for the day?'

Paul drank the last of his coffee and got up from the table. 'To get as much done as I can,' he said. 'I'm just going to grab some tools from the shed.' Paul put his mug in the sink and went out the back.

Carol finished eating and poured the last of her coffee into the sink as Paul came back into the house. 'Better keep moving,' she said. Paul followed her into the bathroom and sat on the edge of the bath while she got ready to shower. He watched her undress and wondered when he'd last seen a woman other than his wife naked. He couldn't remember and didn't know what made him even think of it. He reached out and put the back of his hand against her thigh. She glanced down at him and stepped into the shower.

He started work in the bathroom as soon as Carol had finished showering and by the time she'd come back down dressed for work he had a dozen tiles off the wall and was unscrewing the showerhead. She stood in front of the mirror.

'When can we use the bathroom again?'

'It'll be a few days yet,' he said and kept at the wall. When the walls were clear he knelt and gouged at the grout between the floor tiles with the chisel. He nodded to himself, got up and went into the kitchen. He washed his hands at the sink and lit the stove. The water was on the boil by the time he'd made his sandwich, then he made coffee and went out onto the front verandah to eat.

He got to work on the floor after he'd finished eating. The tiles didn't come up easily or whole and Paul threw the broken tiles into a bucket that seemed to take forever to fill. He kept at it though; he spent the day on his knees wedging the chisel in under the edges of the tiles and when he finally stopped it was almost three o'clock. Carol hadn't come home for lunch; she normally came home for lunch. Paul went to the phone and began to dial the number of the library but he stopped himself. He hung up and went into the spare room and stood beside the desk. After a while he shook his head and went back down the hall to the bathroom.

Paul was back at the desk in the spare room when Carol got home from work.

'Where are you up to in the bathroom?' Carol asked.

'It's ready to tile.'

'Ready to? I thought that you would have made a start on it by now.'

'These things take time.'

'You don't have time,' Carol said and went down the hall. Paul heard her on the phone but couldn't make out what she was saying or who she was talking to. 'I'm going to my sister's for dinner again,' she called from the lounge room. Paul turned in the chair as she walked up the hall past the spare room. 'I'm not sure how late I'll be,' she said as she closed the front door behind her.

Paul stood and watched as Carol got in the car and drove away. He went back to reading and the phone rang a little later. He waited a moment, turned his head to the side, heard it again and got up to answer it. It was Carol calling to say that she would not be home, she was staying at her sister's the night. 'OK,' he said, and hung up. He stood beside the phone for a while, and then went into the kitchen and opened the door of the refrigerator. He closed the door again and went back to the spare room.

He pulled a notebook out of one of the boxes and thumbed through the pages. The pages were lined in pale blue ink but nothing had been written on them. He placed the notebook on the desk and got a pen from the drawer and, at the top of the first page, wrote, *I do not know what I would do if she left me.* Then he got up and went out to the back verandah. He picked up a box of tiles, took them inside and sat them on the floor in the middle of the bathroom. He ripped the lid off the box, took out some of the tiles and laid a row across the floor one way and a second row at ninety degrees to the first. He stood back in the doorway, tilted his head to the side, closed an eye and looked along the wall to see how it all lined up. He got back down on his knees and moved one row of tiles closer to the wall and shuffled the other row to suit. He got up, brushed his palms together and looked at it again and nodded.

He went out and got a bucket and trowel from the shed and began mixing up some tile glue. He half-filled the bucket with water from the garden hose and shook in some adhesive from the bag. Some of the grey powder stayed on the lip of the bucket and Paul tapped the side of the bucket with the toe of his boot to get it in. He used the trowel to work it all into the water and kept adding the powder until he had it right. When the batch of glue was ready he took the bucket inside and put it on the bathroom floor.

Paul set up a string-line across the floor and then he began tiling. He worked his way out from the floorwaste, and by the time he was too tired and hungry to keep going, he'd tiled three-quarters of the floor. He trowelled the last of the glue onto the floor and set another couple of tiles, bedding them in with the heel of his palm. When the last tiles were in place he got up, smoothed the creases out of the leg of his shorts, rubbed at the patches of glue that had begun to dry on his knees, and saw that he'd almost worked himself into a corner.

He took a long step out over the tiles he'd laid earlier in the evening and stood in the hallway looking back into the bathroom. He washed his hands at the kitchen sink, made a sandwich and went back into the spare room. He sat at the desk and opened the notebook and wrote, *I do not know what to tell her.*

They were at the kitchen table. Paul had finished his dinner but Carol was still labouring over hers.

'Not hungry?' he said.

She put her knife and fork on her plate and looked up at him. 'I don't feel like eating,' she said and pushed her plate into the middle of the table.

He picked up both of the plates and took them to the sink.

'Paul,' she said. 'Why aren't you working?'

'I have been,' he said and came back to the table.

'At school, I mean. Why aren't you working at school?'

'I'm just taking some time off.'

'I know, but tell me why. Why are you taking time off? Tell me,' she said. 'I don't want to have to hear it from someone else. You tell me, Paul. Tell me why you need to take time off.'

Carol propped herself up on her elbows. 'I heard some kids talking this afternoon,' she said. 'They were talking about you in the library.'

'What did they say?'

'Just tell me, Paul,' she said. 'I just want to know why you aren't at work.'

'Why? What did they say?'

'What do you think they said? What could they say?'

He put his hands over his face and breathed loudly.

'Tell me, Paul. Please tell me. Why aren't you at work?'

'I need a break,' he said rubbing his thumb over his lips. 'I just need a break.'

'But is it true what they said? Is it?'

He looked at her like he wasn't sure what to say.

'The kids, Paul. The kids.' She leaned toward him. 'Is it true what they said. They said that you hit one of the students,' Carol said. 'Did you?'

He looked up at her. 'What do you think? Do you think that I could do that? Do you?'

'No,' she said. 'But the kids –'

'They weren't there,' Paul said. 'There was only me and the kid that they're talking about.'

'And what did you do?'

Paul scratched at the back of his hand. 'Nothing,' he said. 'I didn't do anything. The kid had a story that he wanted me to read – I'd given the kids an exercise in class a couple of weeks ago and this one kid kept writing, he made a story out of it and he wanted me to read the story.'

Carol got up from the table. 'What was it about?'

'It was about a teacher who couldn't teach anymore because he realised that all he knew was from books and not from life. A man who knew nothing about living.'

'And?' Carol asked. 'And?'

'I thought the story was about me.'

'About you?'

'I thought it was about me. It made sense that way. I asked the kid who he was writing about and he said he'd made it all up. I told him that he was lying,' Paul said. 'I told him that he was lying and that I knew he was writing about me.' He got up from the table and leaned against the sink.

'He laughed. The kid laughed. I could see that he didn't really mean to but I couldn't stand to hear him laugh. I yelled at him. I did want to hit him, I did. I had my hand up to do it but I didn't. I wanted to but I didn't. I promise you that I didn't.'

Carol sat at the table looking at him as if she did not know him at all. Paul turned and stood looking out the window. It was getting dark outside.

'And I was the one who decided I needed to get away from it. It was my decision.'

She looked at him. 'Do you think that you can go back? Could you?'

'I don't know,' he said. 'I don't even know if I want to.'

In the morning, while Carol was next door showering, Paul started getting ready to tile the walls. He drew up the levels and set the string-lines. He laid the first row of tiles and decided to let them sit for a while before he began working his way up the walls. He went out to the shed and got some lengths of timber and, from the spare room, he got a couple of the boxes he'd already finished with and took them into the bathroom. He held the timber against the face of the tiles and pushed the boxes up behind it; he didn't think the tiles were going anywhere but he wanted to make sure of it.

He made a coffee, took it into the spare room and sat at the desk. He read fragments of poems, abandoned stories, false starts of novels. He opened up a book of stories by an American he'd admired when he was at school, an American who had made him want to write even when he didn't think he had anything to write about. He remembered copying down some of the American's stories word for word to see what it felt like to write like that. He remembered that he had kept writing when the story ended; he tried to keep it going for as long as he could, tried to turn the American's stories into his own but each time the story ran out into nothing. Even though they were his own words coming out onto the page, the rhythm became unsettled and fell away, the landscape dissolved, and the characters thinned and vanished. He could see it in his own handwriting, a lightening of the pressure of pen on paper, as though his own words no longer belonged to him. His words had lost conviction.

He opened the notebook again and wrote, *The man waited even though he didn't know what he was waiting for.* Then he scratched out the words and pulled the sheet from the notebook. He looked at the piece of paper and then tore it in half, then in half again and dropped it into the bin beside the desk.

He was still at the desk when Carol came home for lunch. 'How's the bathroom?'

'The first row is on the walls,' Paul said. 'They need to dry for a while. The rest of it should follow on without too much trouble.'

'I hope so,' she said. 'I don't like to shower at Ray and Pam's.'

'Why not?'

'It's not our home,' she said.

'It's nice of them to let us.'

'Yes, it is. But it will be nicer when we can shower at home. Will you get more tiling done today?' Carol asked.

'It needs to dry,' Paul said. 'It takes time.'

'Well it's taking too much time,' Carol said. 'Maybe we should get someone to finish it.'

Paul stood up. 'I'll finish it,' he said and he left the room. He went out and mixed another batch of glue, took it into the bathroom and got to work fixing the tiles to the wall. He stayed with one section of wall and the rows built up quickly. He stepped back from the wall and sat on the edge of the bath. The tiles began to shift under their own weight. Five or six of them fell and broke. 'Damn it,' Paul said. 'Damn it. I can't do this.'

Carol came up the hallway. 'What's wrong, Paul?'

He knelt on the bathroom floor with broken pieces of tile in his hands. 'I can't do it,' he said and looked up at her. 'I can't do it. I just can't.'

'You can, Paul,' she said. 'You're almost there.'

He let go of the pieces of tile. 'I can't,' he said. 'I can't go back. I don't want to go back.'

She just looked at him for a moment and then she got down on the floor beside him and held him. 'You don't have to, Paul. You don't have to go back if you don't think you can.'

The next day Paul was on his knees in the bathroom, rubbing grout into the spaces between the tiles when Carol put a tin of paint down in the doorway. 'I think it should be mauve,' she said.

'What should be mauve?'

'Our bedroom,' she said. 'I think it should be mauve.'

He stopped rubbing in the grout and dropped the sponge into the bucket of grey water. He got up off his knees. 'What's wrong with the way it is now?'

'Tell me,' she said. 'What colour is it now?'

Paul shrugged and looked away.

'See,' she said. 'You don't even know what we've got now.'

'We don't have to change the colour just because I don't know what it's called.'

'No, you're right, Paul,' Carol said. 'We don't have to change it just because you don't know what it is called. We have to change it for a million other reasons. It's drab. It's empty. It's lifeless, Paul.'

Paul rubbed his hands together. Dry grout fell from his palms onto the bathroom floor.

'How long would it take you to repaint the bedroom?' she asked.

Paul looked at her and grinned. 'As long as it takes,' he said.

She drew her lips tight over her teeth and shook her head at him. 'Well I'm not coming back until that mauve is on the walls.'

'What do you mean?' Paul asked. 'Coming back from where?'

'My sister's. The other night I told her how things are at home with you and I said I might want to get away for a night or two.'

Carol went up to the bedroom and pulled a suitcase out from under their bed. Paul heard her opening and closing doors and drawers. He was mixing the last batch of tile grout when she came back down and stopped outside the bathroom. She had the suitcase in her hands.

'You're really going?'

'I am,' she said. 'I'm going to my sister's and I'm not coming back until I can shower in my own home.' She walked out.

Paul heard the car pull away from the gutter. He stood looking down at the tin of paint.

Paul spent the night reading from the boxes and in the morning he began taping them up. He taped the tops of the first couple of boxes, and then he just tucked the flaps in and left it at that. He put one of the boxes up into the cupboard and got back down for the rest. He looked at the boxes on the desk and floor and got back up to get the box down from the cupboard. He took the box out of the spare room and carried it outside and put it on the footpath. He went in and out of the house a dozen times to get all of the boxes out of the house. He stacked them all on the footpath and then went back into the house to get the tin of paint.

Paul sat on the front verandah with the paint between his feet. Carol drove by. He watched her go past then he got up and went inside. He got the pen and notebook from the desk in the spare room and went back out to the verandah.

It feels like I have been waiting all my life for this moment. She is coming home, he wrote and he was going to keep writing until he got it right – the look on her face, the way her smile made him think that she was about to go back on her word and come home before he'd finished painting.

And he was going to keep writing until he knew what it felt like to have the screwdriver under the lid of the paint tin, until he could already hear the sound of the lid peeling back from the lip of the tin, until he could see, really see, and smell the paint as he rolled it onto the bedroom walls. He was going to keep writing until he knew what it felt like to have the rest of his life ahead of him.

Collapsing Under Their Own Weight

Patrick Cullen

Paul leaned against the railing. Below, the sea was grey and green. Waves collapsed under their own weight, churning the water white against the rocks. For an hour he'd watched the swell come in across the sea like dark rolling hills. Clouds built up on the horizon and lightning flared to the south. The wind picked up, driving rain, and the ships turned to face it. Swimmers left the water and surfers made their way up off the beach with their boards under their arms. The car park emptied. Gulls found shelter. Paul waited. They had never met like this.

He folded the collar of his jacket up around his neck and pushed his hands deep into his pockets. A car pulled in behind him and he turned and saw that it was Amy. She reached over and unlocked the passenger door. He got in and leaned over to kiss her. She turned her cheek. 'Aren't you cold?' she said.

'Just wet.'

'How long have you been waiting?'

'Not long,' he said. 'Where's Caitlin?'

'I left her with my mother. She doesn't need to be out in this.'

Paul nodded and leaned forward in the seat. He took off his jacket and put it onto the floor. He ran his fingers through his hair and wiped the water onto his thigh.

'It's been a while since you've seen her,' she said.

'I've been busy.'

'Are you working again?'

He shook his head.

'How's Carol?'

'It's hard to find work at the moment,' he said, leaning back in the seat. 'I'm not sure if I want to teach anymore.'

'Some days I don't think I can face it either, but I do.'

'I can't face it,' he said. 'Not now.'

'Why not? What's wrong, Paul?'

'She's got cancer,' he said.

Amy looked down at his jacket on the floor. The collar was dark where the rain had soaked in. She rubbed her fingertips over her lips.

Paul looked at her like he wanted some sort of answer. 'Carol's got cancer,' he said. 'I thought you needed to know.'

She looked back up at him. 'How is she?'

'They'll operate,' he said. 'We won't really know until after that.'

'I'm sorry,' she said. 'Tell her I'm sorry.'

He looked away.

'Please tell her I'm sorry and that I hope it all works out OK.'

He put his hand to his forehead and held it there.

'She doesn't know,' she said. 'She doesn't know about us, does she?'

'She knows about Caitlin but she doesn't know that you're back in town.'

'I thought she knew. I thought she knew about all of this, about you seeing Caitlin.'

He shifted in the seat.

'You should tell her. She needs to know.'

'Not now,' he said. 'I can't tell her now.'

'I would want to know if I was Carol.'

'But you're not Carol.'

'You do need to tell her about us,' she said.

'And what will I tell her?'

'Just tell her the truth. Tell her that I'm back in town and that you want to see Caitlin.'

He clenched his jaw and looked at her. His lips were pulled tight. 'Does Caitlin know that I'm her father?'

Amy shook her head. 'We're friends, Paul. That's all she needs to know for now.'

A car pulled in beside them. A man got out and put on a wetsuit, took a surfboard off the roof of his car and headed down to the beach. Thunder came in across the sea and the car rocked with gusts of wind. Amy ran the windscreen wipers for a moment. The man waded into the water and paddled out. The rain set in and the man disappeared into the sea.

'You haven't really been her father,' Amy said.

'I could've been,' he said. 'But you left town.'

'You never asked me to stay.'

They sat without talking. The rain stopped for a moment then came back hard again.

'Do you want to be her father now?' Amy said.

'I am her father,' he said.

'You know what I mean,' she said. 'Do you want to be her father? Is that what you want? After all these years, is that what you want?'

He said nothing.

'Is that what you think I want from you? Because I don't want that. I've never wanted that,' she said. 'And I don't think you even know what you want.'

'I want Caitlin to know who I am.'

'And I think you should tell Carol.'

'I will tell her,' he said. 'But I can't tell her right now.'

'You don't want her to know, do you?'

'It doesn't matter.'

'It must matter,' she said. 'Or you would've already told her.'

Paul wound the window down a little. Water ran down the inside of the window and gathered on the sill. 'I need to know about us,' he said.

'What about us?'

'Could there ever be anything between us again?'

She shook her head. 'There's never been anything between us.'

He looked away. His breath condensed on the window. 'I didn't think I would ever see you again,' he said. 'But when I saw you with Caitlin I wasn't sure what I wanted. I think I just want to see her.'

'You can,' she said, putting her hand on his arm. 'I do want you to see her but that's all I want.'

He smiled and shook his head.

'You still love Carol, don't you?'

He nodded. 'It's hard right now but I think we're OK.'

Amy wiped the windscreen with the palm of her hand. 'Where is he?' she said, leaning forward against the steering wheel. 'I can't see him.'

'Who?'

'The surfer. Where is he? His board is there but I can't see him.'

The surfboard drifted in to the beach. The waves pushed it up onto the sand and dragged it back into the water.

'I can't see him,' Amy said. She had her hand on the handle of the door. 'Where is he?'

'There he is,' Paul said, pointing south along the beach. The surfer appeared in the wash and waded to shore. He walked back up the beach, pulled his board out of the water and squatted next to it. He undid the leg rope from his ankle and looked at the end where it had come away from the board. He shook his head and wound the rope around his hand and made a fist of it. He picked up his board and walked back up to the car park. He tied the board back onto the roof of his car, unzipped his wetsuit and rolled it down till it hung around his waist. He wrapped a towel around his waist, kicked out of the legs of his wetsuit and got into his car.

Amy looked at her watch. 'I need to pick up Caitlin. I can drop you home.'

'I'll walk,' Paul said. 'It'll stop raining sooner or later.'

He picked his jacket up off the floor and got out of the car.

Amy leaned across to lock the door. Paul's face was reflected in the glass. He raised his hand briefly, and then let it fall against his side. Amy started the car, waited for a gap in the passing traffic then pulled out and drove away.

The wind dropped. The sun broke through cloud and people came back out onto the beach. Paul headed home. Waves kept collapsing under their own weight.

'And?'

Patrick Cullen

'"And?" What do you mean, "And?"' Paul said, turning away from the sink.

'And do you still love her?'

'We've been through this already.'

'I know we have, but – '

'Well, why do we have to go through it again?'

'Because I don't believe you,' Carol said, crossing her legs at the kitchen table.

'You don't believe me?' Paul shook his head. 'You still don't believe me?'

Carol folded her arms and leaned on her elbows. 'I've never believed you.'

Paul turned back to the sink and put his hands into the water. There was nothing left to do so he let out the water and turned to face her. Water ran off his fingers onto the linoleum. 'Well you shouldn't have to believe me,' he wiped his hands against his shirt. Carol glanced down at the floor. 'It's got nothing to do with you,' Paul said, opening the door of the refrigerator.

'Yes it does.'

'Why does it have anything to do with you?'

'Because I'm your wife,' Carol said. 'That's why.'

'But you weren't then,' Paul said, taking a beer and moving

out past her. He left her alone in the kitchen and went out onto the back verandah and sat on the steps. The concrete was hot beneath his feet; he pulled his toes away from it and dabbed at it until he could take the heat. He looked out across the neighbouring yards. There were lights in windows, shadows moved behind glass and voices said things not meant for him.

The southerly hadn't yet kicked in like they said it would. Paul decided to wait it out until it did. He wouldn't be able to sleep and he knew that Carol wouldn't either. They had eaten without speaking; the scratching of cutlery on their plates was the only thing in the silence between them, and he wished he could have that silence over again. Cupboard doors were opening and closing inside the house and something got broken.

It was quiet for a while, and then Carol came out the back and stood beside him. 'The cicadas have stopped,' she said. 'Too hot even for them.'

Carol stretched Paul's towel out on the verandah railing. 'How was the beach?'

'Good,' Paul said, drinking his beer. 'There were more than thirty ships out there waiting to get into the harbour. You should have seen them all out there going nowhere.'

'I wonder if it's as hot out there on the water as it is in here.'

'I wonder,' Paul cupped his hand against her ankle.

Carol sat next to him on the step and put her head against his shoulder. 'When is this change going to come through like they promised?'

'Who knows?' Paul worked his fingertips in through her hair, moved them in against her scalp. 'It's been a long day.'

Carol nodded and began to cry.

'Would it have helped us if we had some kids of our own?' Paul asked. 'Would it?'

'You know it's no use asking.'

'But would it have helped us?'

'I don't know,' Carol said. 'I really don't know.'

Fruit bats crashed into the fig trees and flapped and fought and fell away to do the same thing further along the street.

Paul and Carol waited on the back step together in darkness for something that neither of them thought would ever come.

That morning, the doctor had told them that he hadn't found any reason why she couldn't carry. 'Some women just can't,' the doctor said, writing her name on an envelope.

'"Just can't",' Carol said. 'That's all you can say? "Just can't."' She stood up and put her palms on the desk. 'I've lost three babies in two years and all you can say is I just can't. I already know that. I already know I can't. I just want to know why I fucking can't.'

The doctor looked up at her then back down at his desk. He shifted his weight in his chair and looked at Paul.

'Is it anything to do with me?' Paul asked.

'No, it's not you,' the doctor said. 'You're not the problem.'

'So now I'm the problem,' Carol said. 'I'm the problem.'

'I'm sorry, I didn't mean that,' the doctor said, putting down his pen. 'But still, I can't find any medical reason why you can't carry a baby to full term.'

Paul reached for Carol's arm but she pulled away. 'Just take me home,' she said.

They drove back toward the freeway. Paul asked Carol if she wanted to eat before they left Sydney but she didn't answer. She pulled her feet up onto the seat and turned toward the window. Her shoes were on the floor on top of the envelope the doctor had slid across his desk as they left his office. Paul just drove.

The traffic slowed as it made its way through the cuttings at Mount White. Three lanes merged into one, slowed to walking pace, then stopped. Workmen chipped away at the rockface, taking out loose pieces of rock. The cutting hung over them.

'Tell me again, how old is she?'

'Eight,' Paul said, keeping his eyes on the road. 'She's probably eight.'

'You've got an eight-year-old daughter that you've never even met.'

'We were young,' he said. 'And then she moved to Sydney with her parents.'

They fell back into silence until Paul said, 'I wish there was something they could do. Something I could do.'

'You've done enough already,' Carol said under her breath.

Paul looked over at her. 'What's that supposed to mean?'

Carol folded her arms and turned away from him again. 'Just take me home.'

They sat and waited for the cars to begin moving again and when they did Paul swerved back and forth between the lanes, accelerating through the traffic.

When they had first talked to the doctor the year before about the two babies she'd already lost, the doctor had asked if they had any children already.

Carol shook her head.

'Yes,' Paul said. 'A daughter.'

The doctor looked across at Carol and then down at his desk. His pen scratched against the paper as he wrote some notes into their file. 'How old is your daughter?' the doctor asked without lifting his head.

Carol stood up and, without speaking, left the room.

They drove home in silence. Paul heard Carol breathing heavily beside him but he didn't look over at her, he just kept driving. When they got home, Paul followed Carol into the kitchen, lit the stove and placed the kettle over the flame.

Carol sat at the table with her head in her hands. After a while she looked up at Paul. Her lips were tight like she was struggling to hold something in. The kettle began to make some noise because it was almost done.

'I can't believe you didn't tell me,' Carol said. 'I'm your wife, Paul. And you didn't even think to tell me this.'

Paul shrugged.

'I shouldn't have to ask,' Carol said. 'You should have told me.'

'I know.'

'What else haven't you told me?'

Paul turned away. 'Nothing,' he said, lifting coffee cups from the hooks beneath the shelf. 'Would it have changed anything?'

'I don't know,' Carol said. 'But at least I would have known.'

Paul turned off the gas and made coffee. 'We were just out of school,' he said, putting the cups onto the table. 'We were camping with friends and she got pregnant. Her parents were moving to Sydney and she went with them. I stayed here to go to uni.' He sat at the table with her. 'I did keep in touch for a while.'

'What about the baby?'

'All I heard was that it was a girl.'

Carol stirred her coffee; the teaspoon rang like a small bell against the edge of the cup. 'Do you ever think about her?' she asked. 'Your daughter?'

Paul breathed out across the top of his coffee. 'Sometimes.'

Paul first saw his daughter in the months before Carol's first miscarriage. As he drove along King Street he saw a woman standing at a corner holding a young girl's hand. He stopped further along the street, watched them cross, and waited on the footpath for them to pass. 'Amy,' he said. 'Amy.'

'Yes – ' she stopped. 'Paul?'

Paul nodded and the corner of his mouth tightened. He looked at the girl and back at Amy. 'Is this?'

'This is my daughter Caitlin.'

The girl smiled at the mention of her name.

'Caitlin, this is Paul. He's a man Mummy used to know.'

'Yes, that's right.' Paul looked at Caitlin. 'Your mum and I used to be friends.'

'Hello, Paul,' Caitlin said. 'Aren't you friends any more?'

Paul glanced at Amy. She looked away.

'Where are you headed?' Paul asked.

'Home,' Caitlin said. 'Would you like to see my room?'

Paul drove them home and Amy invited him inside. Caitlin

showed him her room and the bag she took to school every day. Amy made coffee the way he liked it and they talked. She was a teacher. Her parents had never really settled in Sydney and her mother had moved back to Newcastle after her father died. Her mother had looked after Caitlin when Amy was at university. She loved teaching. She loved kids. She wanted more. She thought about him often.

As he left, she kissed him and asked if he would be back.

He nodded. 'Yes,' he said. 'I can be here again tomorrow.'

As Paul and Carol drove in through the suburbs toward Newcastle they saw boys in school uniforms waiting for buses with surfboards under their arms. 'Let's swim when we get home,' Paul said. 'It'll be nice.'

'Will it? Do you think a swim will fix things?'

'Well it's too hot not to swim.'

'I don't want to swim,' Carol said.

They turned into Laman Street, parked across from their terrace and went inside. Paul dropped his keys onto the kitchen table and opened the refrigerator. 'Are you hungry?' he asked. Carol said nothing and went upstairs. He heard her shut the bedroom door. Paul went out onto the back verandah and got his swimmers and towel off the railing, picked up his keys and left the house.

From the car park Paul saw rows of surfers sprawled out across the swell with their chins pitched up, waiting. Beyond them, a procession of cargo ships stretched out from the harbour entrance to as far south as he could see. Seagulls squabbled over space on the clifftop railing.

Paul walked down to the water at Susan Gilmore Beach and began wading out. A breaking wave pummelled his chest and he let the water drag him along until he was out of breath. He dug his heels into the sand, got up and waded out into deeper water. He dived under, clinging to the bottom as a big set pushed through, and looked up from beneath the water to see the waves turning over on themselves. He felt the changing pressure in his ears and against his skin. He swam out beyond the break and floated on his back until he felt the heat drain from his body.

Paul and Carol waited together on the back step in darkness until the southerly got underway. It crept up on them like a change in mood.

'It's here,' she sighed, looking up into the dark sky.

The wind seemed to come at them from every direction. The trees began to shift and twist with wind and the bats lost their grip. A grevillea scratched against the verandah guttering and a dog barked somewhere along the street. A window sash was pulled up in the house behind and lights went out next door.

Paul felt things shifting and Carol started talking again. He didn't mind talking; they needed to talk. Carol started asking questions again but this time Paul wasn't sure if she really wanted to know what he had to say, and this time he wasn't sure what it was that he would say.

'How would you feel if you saw her again?' Carol asked.

Paul tapped his beer bottle against the edge of the step. He wanted to say: I have seen her. I have seen her more than once and each time I have seen her I have felt something, and I think that feeling might be love, but instead he said, 'I don't know. I don't know how I would feel.'

Mirror, Mirror

Peter Goldsworthy

1.

The shop assistant seems lost for words as Lucy twirls, slowly, in front of the full-length mirror. Reverential silence, or trick of the trade? No need for further flattery is the message, if also a further, more subtle flattery in itself.

Lucy pirouettes again, a much-practised slow-time three-step. The dress *is* breathtaking: red shot-silk in a classic cut, but with a froth of cheeky embroideries. When she takes her eyes from her own image she finds the assistant has vanished, melting away into the rows of hung skirts and gowns as if she were nothing more than an item of clothing herself.

Another twirl, and the assistant has reappeared with a length of mauve silk, which she not so much arranges as pours about Lucy's neck.

'Perhaps with a scarf, madam.'

Lucy pivots on her heels, glancing back into the mirror over her shoulder, before removing the liquid material and handing it back. 'It's lovely – but my partner doesn't like scarves.'

'Perhaps that's because she can't wear scarves herself, madam,' the assistant says.

The words seem so improbable that the shock of them arrives slowly, as if heard on some kind of delay loop.

'I'm sorry?' Lucy eventually gets out, 'I'm not sure if I heard correctly … '

But the assistant has nothing to add, busying herself folding the scarf as if her words had been spoken clearly enough, and can't – or won't – be taken back.

They can certainly be *sent* back. 'My partner is a man,' Lucy informs her.

'Oh,' the woman says, and smiles briefly and melts away into the camouflage of racks and clothes again. This time, Lucy watches her go, less offended by her presumption than curious. The woman carries herself with a studied grace. A dancer's grace? Or the mannered elegance of the catwalk? There is something of the fashion model about those stylised movements, that wire-thin coat-hanger frame, the impeccably made-up face. A model past her use-by-date, perhaps – but by how much? Lucy tries to guess the woman's age. Thirty-five? Forty? Older than *she* is, certainly. In some ways – the thought strikes her – she might be looking into another kind of mirror, at an older, thinner version of herself. Same bobbed black hair, same dark eyes. Cleopatra eyes, Rob likes to call them. And similar build, although what is a prized slenderness in the younger woman has become a little stringy in the older. Too many faddish diets? Too many obsessive gym sessions?

Similar dress sense, also. Lucy steps out of the red silk, and slips back into her own simple black halter-top and trousers. She stands for a moment in front of the mirror, taking that look in – that shared look – uneasy with it for the first time. A come-hither look? Not overtly. Sensual, yes, but constrained by style. Is there something else to it, something she doesn't quite get? Some secret dress code? Does she look like a woman who would want another woman as a partner? Does she – in short – look like a dyke?

The thin assistant is fussing at the counter, still avoiding eye contact. 'Cheque or credit card, madam?'

'Do you take Diners?'

'Of course,' she says, and begins to fold the dress into layers of crepe paper.

The silence soon becomes awkward. 'I love Harry's designs,' Lucy ventures. 'They seem to suit me.'

'They suit you wonderfully,' the woman blurts out, clearly relieved. She swipes the credit card then adds, more hesitantly, 'I hope you didn't take offence at what I said before.'

'Of course not. Not at all. You obviously mistook me for someone else.'

'Um – yes. I'm sorry. I wouldn't normally … '

'Don't give it another thought.'

Or – *please* – another word. The woman manages a smile as she hands across the glossy boutique bag. Good skin, Lucy sees. A little heavy on the Cleopatra eyeliner. Is *that* the code? There are no other clues. Or nothing obvious; nothing butch, and no exaggerated doll-femininity. One slightly disturbing perception: the hair on those thin, feminine forearms is a little thick, in a masculine sort of way. Lucy is taken back to a period of exam stress, at law school years before, when the hair on her own arms had inexplicably thickened. Her doctor had wanted to talk about eating disorders, but she knew it was never that serious, and of course it had passed soon enough.

As she walks back to her chambers, she wonders if the assistant, too, might have felt as if she were looking into a mirror. A flattering mirror in her case, a mirror that revealed a younger version of herself, a young self whose preferences – of course! – might not just be for the same style of clothes.

This last realisation pleases Lucy, a solution to the mystery, and she quickens her step, late for her first afternoon appointment, the boutique bag – *Harry Who?* – bumping rhythmically at her side.

2.

A surprise at home that night: for the first time in months Rob is already there, waiting inside the door to take her things, mock-butler-fashion, as she arrives.

'They finally give you the sack?' she says, kissing him.

He laughs. 'I had a big win today. I wanted to celebrate it with you.'

He has been celebrating already at the Wig & Gown; she can taste it in his kiss even as she smells it on his breath. He sets her valise and boutique bag to one side, and leads her into the kitchen where a half-bottle of wine and two glasses sit on the bench. Still prattling on, he pours out the last of the wine, emptying himself of his news at the same time. 'I couldn't believe that Mutual would blink. Talk about brinkmanship. We were already walking into court … '

'Congratulations,' she gets in as they clink glasses.

'But how was your day?' he finally remembers to ask.

'The usual. Bitter wives, twisted husbands. But a funny thing happened during lunch.'

'Oh?'

'I'd had my eye on a dress. In the window at Harry Who's. It was still there today. Reduced.'

'From extortionate to merely exorbitant?'

'Very funny. Would you like to see it?'

'Before or after you tell me the price?'

'The price is none of your business. You know I always pay for my own clothes.'

He grins, and raises his glass again. 'Not today. Prudential are paying today. Here's to big cheques and fine clothes.' He drains the glass, then sets it aside. 'OK. I'm ready.'

'For the rest of the story?'

'For the dress. A private showing.'

His mood is infectious. She drains her own glass, retrieves the boutique bag and heads upstairs. At the landing she glances back. He has dragged a chair out into the hall, and sits straddling it, facing the foot of the staircase, grinning.

'I want the full staircase effect, please,' he calls up. 'Lucy descending.'

She slips out of her work clothes, pulls on the dress, then stands in front of the mirror, transfixed again.

'I'm waiting,' comes a reminder call from below.

She touches up her lipstick, keeping him waiting. What shoes to wear? She kicks her day shoes aside, black medium heels that are not quite sensible enough for work, but far too sensible for the new dress. One side of the walk-in wardrobe is dedicated to shoes – the Imelda Marcos Room, Rob likes to joke, too often. She runs her eyes over the ranked and serried pairs. Rob's mood is so euphoric that she might even risk wearing the Bruno Maglis that she still hasn't shown him.

A quick brush of her bob, a last smoothing of silk with the palms of her hands, and she steps out onto the landing, one arm theatrically extended, one leg swivelled in front of the other. Mae West in scarlet, she thinks, needing only a cigarette holder.

'You need a cigarette holder,' Rob says, predictably.

She begins to descend, step by mincing step.

'New shoes?' he notices.

'You've seen them before. I bought them in Melbourne. Remember?'

'So many shoes, so little time …' His words trail off with each step that brings her closer. The silk dress has cast its spell of silence again, this time over him.

'I think I'm in love,' he eventually gets out.

'I would hope so.'

'Not with you. With the dress. Can I wear it too?'

'It's not your colour.' She sits on his lap, and presses his head between her breasts.

'So tell me the story,' he says when he surfaces.

'What story?'

'About the boutique. A funny thing happened during lunch, quote, unquote.'

'Later,' she says, feeling the engorgement of his cock through several layers of fabric, his and hers. Excited herself, as much by that slow walk down the steps and the rub of silk against her skin as by him and his desire, she rises and takes hold of his tie, tugging him to his feet.

3.

She tells him the full story as they lie together afterwards, bare human skin and chesterfield leather stickily adherent and pleasantly, if oddly, indistinguishable. The new dress is largely around her neck; she tugs it away from the sticky regions.

'It threw me for a moment,' she says. 'Such a weird thing for her to say … '

'It's not a bad pick-up line.'

'But why me?'

'Must be that lesbian vamp look. I find it a big turn-on myself.'

She laughs, amused, as he nuzzles into her neck. 'So you also think I look like a dyke?'

'She didn't *think* you were a dyke, Luce. She *hoped* you were a dyke. She was trying it on. A test.'

'Which I flunked.'

'You passed mine again,' he says.

'The oral or the prac?'

They laugh together, as much at the foolishness of the banter as at its content, and rearrange their sticky, entangled limbs.

'So what was she like?' he eventually asks.

'What was who like?'

'Don't be disingenous. Your admirer, of course. Did *she* look like a vamp?'

'I thought she looked rather stylish. Too thin, but quite beautiful, in an older sort of way.'

'What a waste.'

'Depending on your point of view.'

'I'm always happy to depend on mine.'

The barrister in him is hard to best in argument, but a year of brutal family law practice has given her an edge – and a vocabulary – that more than compensates for his many more years of criminal law. 'That's a bit last century, Rob. Surely you don't think that *all* women should prefer men?'

'No!' He pauses; she senses a punchline. 'I just think that all women should prefer me!' He laughs loudly, amused with himself. 'I'm very progressive in my attitudes. I don't care what your second preferences are – men, women or well-hung donkeys.'

In the afterglow of sex she can't help laughing with him. 'I'm not enough for you? You want other women?'

'I want the *idea* of others, maybe.' Another pause; he is thinking it through, perhaps for the first time. 'I've always felt weirdly possessive about women – *all* of them. Total strangers included. A wedding ring glimpsed on a tram, a photo in the paper of some beauty hitching herself to a pig – there's always a pang of disappointment, of something *missed.*'

'You sound like a megalomaniac.'

'I sound like a man.'

'My case rests.'

He laughs again. 'You might have a point. Look at history. Absolute power corrupts sexual appetite absolutely.'

'Always?'

'Always. Given half a chance the first thing every king, emperor or village chief does is get himself a harem.'

'Even if he has to start a religion to justify it.'

'Women *are* the religion. My favourite wanking fantasy as a teenager was being the only man left on the planet – with *all* the women.'

'We'd tear you apart.'

'Yes, please,' he says, then adds, encouraged by her laugh, 'I know which bit you'd tear off.'

Prompted, she reaches down for that bit, soft now, and a little tacky to the touch as its stickiness dries out. She plays idly with it as he talks on.

'You must have had similar fantasies, Luce.'

'Not really. Or not about particular men.' She pauses, thinking back. 'I fantasised about being a different woman sometimes.'

He finds this difficult to believe. 'You didn't like being you?'

'When *I* was a teenager I was an ugly duckling. In a world of beautiful swans. Films, magazines, billboards – beautiful swans everywhere, wearing beautiful feathers.'

Her own red silk feather is rucked high about her neck and shoulders. She had longed to own such clothes as a girl. In her drab, Methodist bush town there had been little place for such luxury – except in magazines. She had pored over her mother's collection – the new royalty of glitz as well as the old royalty of blood. She had yearned to look like that, to be like them – and somehow, almost without noticing, the miracle had occurred: while her head had been cocooned in her law school books, she had morphed into the swan of her adolescent fantasies.

'Why is it,' Rob is asking, 'that men's magazines are full of pictures of women, but so are women's magazines?'

'A small difference might have escaped your notice: the women wear clothes in women's magazines.'

'Only to hide their bones. Why do women like to look at *emaciated* women?'

'It's what men like. An image you force on us.'

He snorts. 'Men like women with a bit of flesh on their bones. You never see those supermodel types in men's magazines.'

'I guess clothes hang better on skinny women.'

Her own thoughts drift on, and further away. The face of the thin shop assistant swims back into focus; she sees again that dark gaze lighting on her, appreciating her. She feels a slight thrill in the skin of her arms at the idea of the woman wanting her, wanting to do – what? Step into the changing room with her? Kiss her? Touch her, *finger* her? Unsettled, she feels the need to talk about it again, to further unravel the puzzle, or at least talk these disturbing feelings to a standstill.

'It *was* a strange conversation, don't you think?'

'Which conversation?'

'In the shop. About the scarf.'

'Very strange. What on earth made her think you would look good in a scarf?'

Lucy chuckles, agreeably; he extracts an arm from the mix of their limbs and reaches for the television remote.

'Perhaps it was my choice of words. Perhaps some people assume that "partner" means gay partner?'

'Gay partners probably assume it.'

'If I'd said "my husband", do you think she would have come on to me?'

English footballers are colliding on the television; a crowd is roaring its love for, and hatred of them. 'Maybe you'd better go back and ask her. But make sure you leave your Diners card at home.'

'I thought you had a big win today?'

'A one-dress win. And maybe a pair of shoes.'

His tummy rumbles, noisily; despite his slight paunch, she can feel the vibration as much as hear it.

'Well put,' he says, addressing his stomach. 'My thoughts exactly.'

'It's your turn to cook,' Lucy tells him.

'I cooked last night.'

'*I* cooked last night. You cooked Tuesday night.'

'Then I vote we eat out. Somewhere special. To celebrate. And you can wear the red dress.'

'I was going to wear it tomorrow night.'

'Wear it both nights,' he says, but they are still too torpid to move. He turns up the volume of the football; her thoughts return yet again to the shop, and the strange woman.

'I thought I might do a David Beckham,' he is saying somewhere.

'Mmmm?'

'Apparently he waxes his scrotum.'

His own unwaxed scrotum is still nestled in the palm of her hand; she has been jostling his testes as if they were a pair of worry-balls. Clinkers, is the term she has heard somewhere recently, and liked.

'You haven't been keeping up with the gossip pages,' he tells her. '*That* was the proof of the affair. The intimate detail that only a lover could have known. '

He nuzzles into her; his hands begin to re-explore her body. Fondling those worry-balls might be relaxing for her, but the effect is exactly the opposite on him.

'Wait,' she says. 'I want to take the dress off this time.'

'Only if you do it slowly.'

She stands in front of him, and removes the dress from her upper body, luxuriating again in the liquid texture of the fabric. He watches her with some ardency, and her skin prickles as she remembers the thin woman's dark eyes feasting upon her in similar fashion.

'If I were a woman I'd prefer to be a dyke,' he says, back at his most predictable again.

She is about to cast the dress aside when she notices the damp patch.

'Shit!'

'What?'

'There's a stain.'

His glance moves reluctantly from her body to the dress in her hands, and the wet patch proffered accusingly towards him.

'I never had sex with that woman, your honour!' he jokes, but she has already turned away, hurrying through the house in the direction of the laundry.

4.

She walks past the boutique on Monday morning – as on every other weekday morning – on her way from her parking-bay to chambers. It's early – 8 a.m. – and the store is closed, but the window displays are lit and she pauses as if to inspect them. She presses her nose to the glass, peering beyond the array of winter coats, but the assistant is nowhere to be seen inside. She walks on, valise in one hand, the red dress in its boutique bag in the other. It had been a mistake to try to clean the silk herself; the fabric is now water marked. She turns in at the drycleaners next to her chambers, a hole-in-the-wall Lebanese franchise whose elderly owner always treats her, flirtatiously, as his most valued customer.

Which she possibly is.

'Mrs Lucy! I thought you had abandoned me!'

'Because I hadn't been in for three days, Najaf?'

'Four, Mrs Lucy. Four. I have been keeping count.'

She spreads the dress across the counter, and he whistles, appreciatively. 'This is new! I haven't seen *this* before.'

'Worn once.'

She flips the hem and shows him the water mark; he slips on a pair of glasses, and scrutinises the tiny disaster area.

'Naughty girl. You tried to clean it yourself.' He peers up at her over the rims. 'What did you spill?'

She is ready for the question; it isn't the first time. 'Glue.'

His smile is enigmatic. Does he believe her? 'No problem, Mrs Lucy.' He wags a playful finger. 'You always have such beautiful things. You should look after them better. You'd like it today?'

'Please.'

Client meetings carry her through the morning; a difficult settlement hearing consumes most of the afternoon. Rewarding herself with an early minute, she escapes the oppressive emotional atmosphere of her chambers at four, only to find herself – without really thinking about it – standing outside the boutique again.

Is the gravitational force that tugs at her nothing more than curiosity? She hesitates at the open door as the thrill of adrenaline courses through her forearms again, electric in its intensity and brevity. She knows the feeling well, although usually from standing too close to cliff edges, or sitting at the windows of revolving restaurants. Just thinking about heights, even in bed, at night, can bring that same adrenaline tingle. But here, this afternoon, she is at ground-level, and the only way to fall is sideways, in through an open door.

Thumbing through a magazine behind the counter is a shop assistant she hasn't seen before, a shop-girl really, a teen ager trying hard to wear a look of bored superciliousness beyond her years. Complex feelings again flood through Lucy – relief, but also a measure of disappointment. She tugs an item out from the nearest rack and pretends to inspect it.

'Looking for something in particular?'

'Just browsing.'

'Sing out if you need help.' A brief, ritual smile, and the girl returns to her magazine.

Lucy moves along the rack, tilting items out at an angle for brief inspection, lifting one or two completely from the rail.

She moves closer to the counter, within casual chatting range. 'I bought a dress here last week. I was looking at a scarf as well ... '

The girl lifts her eyes reluctantly from a fashion spread. 'You'd like to see it again?'

'The other assistant isn't here today?'

'Which one?'

'Dark eyes. Wears a bob. Fortyish, but rather attractive. Size 8.'

Too much detail? The girl seems more interested now, even knowing. Lucy's heart skips a beat. Does she know about her older colleague? Does she think that *I* ... ?

'Sounds like Joan,' the girl says.

It doesn't to Lucy. Surely lesbians – especially lesbian ex-models – should have exotic names like Sabrina, or Desdemona. Or butch names like Red, or Biff, or Charlie.

'Joan's not here today,' the girl is saying. 'But perhaps I can help. The scarves are this way ... '

'I don't have a lot of time. I thought – she would remember the dress ... '

A definite smirk in the girl's smile. 'You'd prefer to come back and see Joan?'

'It might be easier. She'll be here tomorrow?'

'And the next day. And the day after that.' Brazen cheek now. 'Would you like to leave a message?'

Lucy can feel the heat rising in her face. 'That won't be necessary,' she says, and turns on her heel and walks out before the flush reaches full bloom. Out in the street, she is embarrassed mostly with her own lack of cool. How can a shop-girl with a fuck-you manner get under her skin when hardened family lawyers and curmudgeonly judges have no chance at all? Flustered, she is almost at the parking-station when she remembers the drycleaning. She glances at her watch: 5.30. Too late? She turns and hurries back.

Najaf is standing outside his shop, anxiously glancing up and down the street. 'I thought perhaps you had forgotten,' he says, beaming at the sight of her.

'I'm sorry to keep you back,' she says, as he follows her inside.

'For you, my dove, of course I wait.'

The dress hangs from a rail near the counter. He lifts the clinging hem of its clear plastic sheath and allows her to inspect the cleaned silk.

'You wear it to work tomorrow? You wear it for me?'

'I don't think I'll ever wear it again. It's too beautiful to wear. I think I might just frame it.'

She is home before Rob; no big win today, apparently. Monday is his night to cook, which usually means he will arrive with boxes of Thai or Chinese, or empty-handed and suggesting a meal out. She opens the day's mail, then settles at her escritoire in the study, checking briefs for the following day. Out of the blue the thought strikes her that the dress might have shrunk in the process of cleaning, and although this has never happened before – Najaf likes to talk of himself as an 'artist' – she slips out of her work clothes on the spot, slides the dress from its rustling sheath, and pulls it on.

Lacking a mirror in the study, she climbs the stairs to the master bedroom. Of course there is no sign of shrinkage – where did that absurd notion come from? Displaced anxiety? If so, that anxiety is calmed merely by looking at the dress, at herself *in* the dress, as if contemplating some aesthetic ideal, a perfect match of two forms. She slips the rest of her underclothes off – pantyhose, knickers, bra – relishing the feel of the dress alone, the purity of silk and nothing else against her skin. Barefoot, she descends the stairs to resume her work.

'Are we due out somewhere?'

Preoccupied, she hadn't heard the door. Rob is standing in the hall, watching her, puzzled.

'The dress,' he explains.

'It was your turn to cook. So I assumed we were eating out.'

He lifts the plastic bag in his hand and dangles it at shoulder height; the rich aromas of coriander and ginger reach her.

'All dressed up with no place to go,' he says.

He sets the food down on the hall-stand and steps forward and kisses her warmly on the mouth. He doesn't want to stop; she pushes herself free.

'No more stains, Rob.'

'We can take the dress off,' he says, and seats her on the bottom steps, and kneels before her, and begins to run his lips and tongue over her bare feet, around and between her toes first, then the soft insteps. She tugs the dress over her head and casts it aside, he lifts his head and smiles joyously at the sight of her instantly naked body.

'You *were* waiting for me,' he says, and she shivers, deliciously, as he runs his tongue higher, tickling her calves. 'I told you I'd make a good dyke,' he says, and spreads her lips with his fingers, and begins to lick her, to caress her, with his tongue. His nose is in her pubic hair, his words muffled, 'Anything she can do I can do better.'

Is it his playful talk that prompts her, or allows her – just for a moment – to imagine that it *is* the woman whose mouth and lips and tongue are working upon her? The thrilling force of the fantasy jolts her, she grinds her pelvis into his face and cries out at the rush of pleasure.

Is he aware of what he has done as he lifts his mouth from her, and pulls her down onto the carpet beneath him?

'Of course she can't give you what you love best,' he says in a different, harder voice, 'She can't do *this* to you.'

And he enters her, and for the next few minutes she is lost, gasping and clutching, in the familiar, and the masculine. And it *is* what she loves best, at least for the moment, and if only because the power of the present is such that each time, at the time, the here and now of particular sex seems the best there could possibly be.

5.

8 p.m. Friday. Late-night shopping. Standing outside the boutique with a clutch of other designer label bags in her hands, Lucy wonders why she avoided the place for the rest of the week, even to the extent of walking the long way round to

work. For although the thin woman stands at the counter again, chatting on the phone, the gravitational pull of that doorway seems to have lost force; if anything Lucy feels a push in the other direction, away.

At least the woman can't see her, lurking outside in the evening shadows. Or can she? As if growing aware that she is being watched, the woman – Joan – begins to turn, and Lucy averts her gaze, and hurries away.

'Lucy!'

At first she ignores the call behind her, and the quick clatter of high heels. Plenty of Lucys in the world.

'Lucy? Lucy Byrne?'

Now a hand is plucking at her elbow; she has no choice but to turn and face the music. 'You know my name?'

'It was on your credit card.'

The woman is smiling, tentatively. Has she put on weight, or is it the smile that fattens her gaunt face, adds an extra ounce or two of flesh? 'I'm glad you came back, Lucy.'

'I haven't. I was just passing ... '

'Kylie said you'd been in on Monday. Asking after me.'

'I was asking after *the scarf*.'

'I felt so – relieved. I'd hate to think that anything I said, or did ... I just wanted you to feel, well, *comfortable* coming back.'

The hand lingering on Lucy's wrist feels anything but comfortable. Her eyes move to that hand, then away again; the woman smiles and leaves it there.

'Have you time for a drink? I'm about to shut up shop.'

A lurch of her heart. 'I have to meet Rob.'

'Of course. The, um, partner.' A tongue-in-cheek smile? Cheeky, certainly. Her fingers slip lower and entwine with Lucy's; their touch is so exquisite she can barely breathe.

'Come inside. Please. Just for a few minutes. You can try on anything you like. In private.'

Lucy's heart is lurching now from beat to beat; the flush rising. 'I might try that scarf again,' she manages to stammer. 'But not today, Joan.'

Another smile. 'You know my name too.'

'Kylie mentioned it.' She frees her hand from the woman's grasp, but is unable to tear away her eyes.

'Come tomorrow then. Come at noon – closing time. We'll have the shop to ourselves.' A pause, a knowing look. 'I have something you really must try.'

As Lucy stands frozen to the spot, and speechless at the audacity of this, the woman leans forward, cheek first, as if to offer an air-kiss, but instead meets her lips softly, and briefly.

Lucy starts back, but the woman is already walking away, and it seems – watching that black, trim figure, the bob of dark hair – that she might be watching herself walk away. The feeling is oddly vertiginous, a mild out-of-body experience. Except she is still very much *in* body; the pressure of the kiss, and the tingle of those fingers against hers, remains. She glances about, but no one seems to be watching, and even if they are, will surely think only that these women are sisters, affectionate sisters.

Rob is waiting in their usual café near the cinemas, a newspaper and two coffees on the table before him, one half-drunk. 'You're early, Luce. Your coffee is still warm.'

Not as warm as her face. Her heart is still pounding; her skin tingling, and nowhere as thrillingly as the palm of her hand where she can still feel a phantom pressure of the woman's fingers.

'You're wearing scent,' he says as she brushes her cheek against his.

'A sampler.'

He stares at her, puzzled. 'But you're allergic to scent.'

'It was just a dab.' She glances at the open newspaper. 'What movie are we seeing?

'I was just looking. What's your preference?'

'Feel-good.'

'Tough day?'

'Tough week.'

'The new Coen brothers' is a feel-good.'

'Sounds perfect.'

'It's about a divorce lawyer. Is that light enough?'

He grins, she smiles back. His repartee is light entertainment in itself, so light in content that it can often be vacuous. But its style is something more durable, and familiar, and brings her back, brings her *down* to earth, to the soft, nourishing loam of their life together.

She chuckles. 'Maybe we should just stay in and watch the football.'

'Fine by me,' he says. 'If you put on the red dress when we get home. And a few more dabs of perfume – in the right places.'

6.

He is up early at his desk in the morning; she lingers in bed with the Saturday papers, and allows herself to be brought a relay of coffees, and fruit in bowls. After an hour or so, she tries to sleep again, *wanting* to sleep, if less through tiredness than the need to time-travel safely past noon.

'Let's go somewhere for lunch,' she says, when Rob brings up the third coffee.

'Some of us have work to do. And we're having dinner out, remember? Then the theatre.'

'What about that movie? We could take in the matinee. You need a break.'

He bends to kiss her on the forehead. 'You had your chance of a movie last night. And you blew it.'

'I blew *some*thing,' she says, but he is already heading back to the study, too busy for sexual word-play this morning.

She reaches again for the papers. She has exhausted the film and book reviews, the op-ed pieces. She completes the cross-quiz and the cryptic crossword, then to no likely end-purpose begins to circle properties in the real estate lift-out.

'Still in bed?' Rob asks from the door, surprised.

'Still at your desk?'

10.30 a.m. She wraps herself in the doona and shuts her eyes again, but she is too high on caffeine to sleep, and soon Rob reappears in the doorway with yet another fix of the drug.

'Maybe I *could* find the time for a movie.'

The question is rhetorical, she supplies the necessary answer: 'No. You need to work.'

'Then go without me.'

'By myself?'

'Ring Jen. Or Heather. You can't stay in bed all day.'

11 a.m. An hour till boutique closing time. She drains the coffee dregs, rises and stretches and examines herself, naked, in the wall-mirror. A longer than usual beauty sleep has done her no harm, although there is not enough time to wash her tangled bed-hair. She has, she tells herself, a well-fucked look, and with good reason. So why – now that she is on her feet – does she still feel the tug of the boutique. She tries to analyse the attraction, to reason it to a standstill. Does her own body, reflected in the mirror, offer the clue? She has grown to love this sleek swan which for so many years repelled her – she has grown, at least, to love living *inside* it, to love it from the inside out. She has, in some sense which seems to her more complicated than mere vanity, acquired the taste of herself. Is this, then, the fascination of the shop assistant? To be kissed and touched by herself; to *touch* herself? But she can do that – *has* done that countless times, if less often since living with Rob. He touches her as much as she needs – exactly as often as she needs, it sometimes seems. He pleases her more than any man has pleased her in the past, and in ways that still surprise her.

Is the lure of the forbidden the attraction? But forbidden by whom, these days? The lure of the exotic, then? But why *this* exotic, and why now? She has never wanted to have sex with a woman before – unless masturbation counts. She loves men; she has always loved – and wanted – men. She loves Rob, and wants him daily; she has placed him above all other men.

Is she bored then? Is she – and this is the least disturbing thought – merely curious?

11.15 a.m. Best to keep moving while also keeping thinking. She can call a halt at any time, meanwhile why not keep her options open? She takes a shower, washing off the smell of bed, sponging away the smell of sex. Routine shower habits these, but the thought strikes her that she is also washing away the man-smell. Wash that man right out of my cunt? She tries to put the surprising thought out of her head, but it seems only to ripple down through her body, like a shiver.

Back in front of the mirror, she tugs her bed-hair up into a punkish spout, chokes it with elastic. Rapid lipstick application next, a quick highlighting of the Cleopatra lashes. But not too much. Nothing vampish. What, now, to wear? There is no time to dawdle; she pulls on jeans and a plain black top, flat heels.

'Nice hair,' Rob says, sarcastically, as she steps into the study to kiss him goodbye. 'Don't do anything I wouldn't do,' he adds, and her heart lurches again; significance now in everything.

Too much traffic on the roads, too many slow lanes, too many red lights. The lower floors of the parking-station are fully occupied; she drives around and around and higher and higher. Five minutes to noon by the time she squeezes, starting to panic, into a disabled bay. Her watch is not known for quartz-quality accuracy; hopefully it's fast. No time to wait for the lift; she hurries down the fire-escape stairs, flat heels clattering on metal. The stairwell is steep, several times she catches at the rail, lest she fall. Vertical gravity this, real gravity with real dangers. Worse dangers? Hard to tell as she bursts out through the exit door onto the street, and into the tug of the other, powerful gravity.

The town hall clock is tolling noon as she emerges, blinking, into bright sunlight. She walks quickly, breaking into a shuffling run for the last block.

In vain; the doors of the shop are closed, the interior beyond the lit windows dark. Breathless, she presses her nose to the glass and peers inside. Movement in the gloom somewhere, a vague vibration. She raps on the glass, then again, more forcefully.

She is about to turn away when she senses the sound of approaching footsteps inside. She has been rushing too much to feel any thrill, now the thrill itself comes in a rush. Her heart stops, perhaps for good; she can barely breathe as the door opens a few inches.

But it's the younger woman – the snooty girl Kylie – who peers out through he narrow gap with a pained look on her face.

'We've just closed.'

'I can see that. I'm sorry. But I had an appointment. At noon.'

The girl shrugs, unconcerned. 'You must have the wrong day. We always close at noon on Saturdays.'

Lucy slips the toe of her shoe into the gap, which is threatening to shut in her face. 'No. It was today. I was here last night. The assistant said today. At noon.'

'Ah.' An odd, fleeting disturbance in the girl's face – knowingness? Amusement? 'That would have been with Joan.'

Lucy tries to peer past the girl into the gloom of the shop. 'Is Joan here?' That she is making an idiot of herself, arriving flushed and eager and out of breath, is no longer of any concern.

'Are you OK?' the girl asks. 'You seem – breathless.'

'I was running late.'

'Are you a friend of hers?'

'Of course not. I'm just a customer. I came about a scarf. Last night. She said she'd be here today.'

The girl is smiling now, but a controlled, only faintly supercilious smile. 'Joan doesn't work here anymore.'

'Since last night?'

'It happened very quickly.'

'She resigned?'

Another careless shrug. 'I don't really know a lot about it. But I know there have been complaints from customers. Apparently it all came to a head this morning.'

Silence.

'I could give you her private number. If it's so important to you.'

'Why on *earth* would I want her private number?'

'Hey – I just work here. No need to bite my head off.' The girl looks her up and down. 'You've been in before, haven't you? *Now* I remember. You were asking for her then.'

'I was asking about the scarf.'

'We open again on Monday. Perhaps I can help you with the, ah, scarf,' the girl says, and looks her insolently in the eye.

'Somehow I doubt that very much. I don't think *you* would have a clue.'

The girl glances down at the foot wedged in the door, and back up, but Lucy keeps it there a moment longer, as if to make a further point.

'Do you *mind?*'

She does mind, and she keeps it there a moment longer before allowing the door to close, but her small triumph is forgotten as the sound of giggling comes through the shut door, a high-pitched but oddly hollow sound, not unlike the tinkling of coat-hangers in an empty robe.

Then the girl's face appears in the window, still smirking, and Lucy turns on her flat heels and flees, but flees slowly, placing each foot in front of the other carefully and deliberately, husbanding her dignity despite the tears of frustration that fill her eyes and blind her to the passing bargain hunters and gatherers carrying home their Saturday morning booty.

The Only Damage

Melissa Goode

I arrive in Bathurst from Sydney in the late hours of the afternoon. The sky is fading pink; the Open sign in shop windows is being turned to Closed. A cricket game ends with men in whites walking slowly across the field to the parking lot. People have polished themselves a little, hair still wet from the shower; purchasing cigarettes and alcohol and chips from the bottle shop. This is a country town preparing itself for a Saturday evening. People wander into the pub, into the video shop, into the local Chinese restaurant. I grew up on the outskirts of a town like this.

His parents live in Bathurst in a two-storey blonde brick house in town. They built it in the late sixties after their honeymoon in Tweed Heads. He rolled his eyes when he told me that, and I was not sure whether he was rolling his eyes at their having a honeymoon, or that it was in Tweed Heads. I would have loved to have a honeymoon with him and I would not have cared where it was; it could have been in his parents' backyard and it would have been lovely.

I pull up out the front of his parents' house and not a damn thing has changed.

*

The hands that he put all over me were stained with ink rather than dirt. The first time we fucked he read me a poem. He had grabbed the book out of my school bag. It was a poem that I was studying for the HSC; Keats, 'La Belle Dame sans Merci'. I thought I understood the poem after he read it to me. The only part I remember now is, 'And there I shut her wild, wild eyes/With kisses four' which of course is what he did. The fact that I represented death was not entirely lost on me. I just thought it was cool. He wrote the words on my arm. Men don't read poetry to their women where I come from.

*

I do not see him when I first walk into his room. The walls are lit with a pink orange glow from a lamp in the corner. The afternoon outside is deciding upon a storm; thunder rumbles nearby and only muted light comes through the window. On the unmade bed there is the suitcase gaping open; evidence of the journey made to here, its innards spilling.

Amidst the clutter on the desk is his heavily bent head. All I can see is the pale nape of his neck caught in the lamplight, and the stoop of his bony shoulders. It is the posture of a person burdened, or awaiting punishment; the posture of a writer writing. Above his head the same pictures are pinned, overlapping each other: pictures of naked women; pictures of religious deities; pictures of places in Europe, South America and India. Places I presume he has now been to. The room smells of cigarettes and the mustiness of a place that has been shut up for some time. Waiting.

The world has peeled away and there is only this room. But then his mother's voice clamours up the stairs, 'Sean? Honey. I've sent Rita on up.' I imagine she stands at the foot of the stairs, holding his shirt by the collar; the shirt on which she was sewing a button when I rapped on the back screen door.

He swings around distractedly; not the whole body, just the torso and startled face. His dark hair is longer, and falls over his ear with the movement. He looks the same after three years, but thinner; the bones in his face are more pronounced, and his eye sockets seem deeper.

'Are you writing about revolution while your mother mends your shirt?' I ask.

He offers me an uplifted corner of his mouth and I can see that he is relieved that I am starting with sarcasm and not with anger.

'Rita,' he says, and the word resounds with warmth, as if he has opened his arms to me. But he hasn't; he is getting to his feet awkwardly and I cannot help but notice that his clothes are hanging off him. I try not to stare. He drops a short kiss onto my cheek, but then thinks better of it and draws me against his ribs. He smells the same. I breathe deeply and forgive myself for this. I think about all the water under the bridge for us to be hugging in his old bedroom in his parents' house.

'I was thinking you might be coming by,' his mother had said, holding the screen door open for me. I recognised the dress she wore, white with aqua palm trees splashed across it, showing her knobbly shoulders and elbows and the faint track of her sternum. Her hair dyed blonde above an ageing face. Our eyes connected and she looked at me as if she knew me. As if she had me all worked out. The sewing scissors, spools of cotton and some needles lay on the kitchen table like instruments being used in an operation. I recognised the clothes slumped over the back of the kitchen chair as his clothes: white button-through shirts, a green silk shirt, and a black velvet jacket. Mending. It was certainly the time for mending.

He holds me at arms' length and openly studies me; eyes like green glass. My dark hair is longer now and no longer pulled roughly from my face, my fitted fairy floss pink dress shows the puppy fat I have lost, my feet are bare, slender, with red toenails. I had followed the ritual of the household and left my shoes at the door. His feet are bare too, pale and edged in lilac: cold. I remember holding those feet. I remember him washing me. I remember him dressing me up. I remember his hands twisted in my hair, binding him to me.

He does not say anything. His hand slides around my waist

to rest at the small of my back, and his other hand takes my hand and he leads us in classic dancing style.

'What are you doing?' I ask, and look up at him. His smile is only centimetres from me.

'This is the last thing we did before I left. Your brother, Marty's wedding. Sinatra singing "It had to be you".' He hums a couple of bars. I remember a few things that came after that dance but do not say this; instead I untangle my fingers from his.

His fingertips touch my shoulder, 'You've been in the sun,' he says, watching his fingers leave white imprints on my skin, which then disappear into the dark pink of my sunburn.

'For the last three years,' I fling the words at him, and take a step backwards.

He turns and fumbles about at the desk. It's not too early, he mutters to himself, grabbing a bottle of scotch and two used glasses.

'Yes. Paris doesn't get as much sun,' he says, lightly, 'Although the food is excellent if you have money. Or so I am told.' He laughs in a way that I do not recognise, as if he is a man of small talk.

He gestures for me to sit on the chair at the desk; a 1960s black vinyl kitchen chair. The seat is still warm. He settles himself at the end of the bed. On one knee he balances a saucer that is already littered with butts. He hands me a glass of scotch. I can see the imprint of his lips on the glass from where he has drunk. I bring the glass to my lips where he had sipped from, and take in a soothing, hot mouthful. When we were teenagers Sean would come over to our house to stay, a friend of Marty's. I would carry Sean's dinner plate into the kitchen and slide his still-warm fork into my mouth. Old habits die hard.

'Ask me whatever you want to ask.' His serious face splits into a smile, 'Then we can get a beer at the pub.'

Then 'cheers' and our glasses chink together.

'I brought the scotch back from Scotland myself,' he offers, holding up the glass to the lamplight. An amber meniscus.

'I wasn't going to ask you about the scotch.' I manage.

He looks at me warily, perhaps changing his mind about his offer. But he is tethered to the bed with his glass of scotch, a cigarette and some sense of obligation.

'I went everywhere. Mostly stayed in Paris,' is how he begins telling the story of his travels. 'Of course, there is nowhere like home,' he concedes, giving me a lopsided, apologetic smile.

I remain silent and wait for him to fill in the spaces.

He looks down at his feet, 'I don't remember much,' he says, softly. Lying.

I flick some torn nailpolish from my fingernails and for a while it's the only sound. But then he clears his throat, 'My friend died,' he taps ash from his cigarette into the saucer.

'Who are you talking about?' I ask, needlessly. I know exactly whom he is talking about. I have heard the gossip.

He looks at me vacantly, 'Marianne. I am talking about Marianne.'

'You don't have to tell me about her,' I say. But he ignores this and begins the sorry tale. The words have already been chosen; it is a story he has had to tell a few people. It is possibly the same story that he told the police: the last night of her life. An English girl, Marianne, took drugs and got behind the wheel of a car and died in a car accident just outside London, killing another person as well, an elderly man. Sean was in the car but he survived; a broken collarbone was the only damage.

I listen to his words as one listens to background music. I hear his brother and father arriving home from their sixth day of labouring of their six-day working week; the dumping of lunchboxes and thermos flasks on the kitchen table. Their short barking words linked with his mother's chatter and instructions. I hear dinner being prepared, the sizzle of meat in a frypan, the pounding of a potato masher in a saucepan. I hear the rain start with loud splats on the corrugated iron roof of the shed out the back, and lightning shatter the sky. Sean raises his voice over the racket. I hear his deep intake of breath between sentences. He may as well be describing his own death. For all his writing, he proved to be a dreadful correspondent. 'So that is why I am back,' and finally the words stop.

I feel a weak smile on my face, and wonder if coming up here I left my self-respect at the door with my shoes. The empty glass that I place on the desk makes a resounding clunk as it connects with the wood, like the sound of a gavel.

'I had better get home,' I announce, and straighten up out of the chair.

He looks up at me astonished, 'Why don't we get a beer? Don't go.'

My footsteps are soundless as I leave the house. His mother is crouched in front of the oven, spooning juices over meat. I suspect she is still cooking his favourite meals even a fortnight after his arrival. She does not see me leave, or if she does, she ignores me. I slip my thongs back on, and walk around the side of the house to the street. Sean is already there, leaning against the car with his arms folded. His bare feet, crossed, white against wet asphalt. The sun emerges and the road becomes golden, reflecting the sky.

'Take me with you,' he says, almost jokingly.

I hear the keys jingling in my hand before I realise that I am shaking.

He says my name, kindly.

'I did not want to hear about Marianne. How could you think I would want to know?' I say, quietly.

'I wanted you to know what happened. I did not want there to be secrets between us.'

'Secrets,' I mutter, but bite my tongue.

His father hollers out through the front door that dinner is ready. I move to push past him to get into the car. He grabs my wrist in a vice-like grip. The violence of it sends a helpless thrill of excitement through me. Behind his head the sky changes to green and it will rain at any moment. He smiles and releases me one finger at a time. Something in his smile makes it more like a leer. His dark hair swings over one eye, and he is the first to drop his gaze. He lets go of my wrist.

'What happened to you while I was gone?' he asks.

*

It had to be you. Someone had decorated the packing shed with paper lanterns and streamers, and tea-light candles lined the windowsills. The concrete floor had been painted pale pink. The trestle tables were covered with white linen tablecloths, borrowed from someone. It was still the packing shed. I could detect rotten apples beneath the smell of the roasting pig. I could hear the rats scuffling in the roof under the crooning of Frank Sinatra. Marty and his new wife sat at the main trestle table obligingly kissing every thirty seconds when anyone clinked their knife against their glass; she getting drunk on Midori and lemonade, and he on Bourbon and Coke.

Sean had taken off his jacket, loosened his tie and undone the first few buttons of his white shirt; an invitation. Outside there was laughter, and the rattle of cans and balloons being strung up to Marty's old Holden which was playing the part of Wedding Car. Inside, a glass smashed on the concrete floor; my slightly drunk fourteen-year-old cousin stared at the mess, appalled. Sean had one arm around my waist and his other hand held mine. He smelt my skin. He made pretend puking actions in reference to the music. He whispered, 'We could give them a show.' Nobody else was dancing. His hand disappeared into my hair, wandered down to my shoulder and rested dangerously close to my breast. 'I love you best,' he confided in a damp whisper into my ear. From Sean McIntyre this was the most I could hope for, and I smiled.

*

While I was helping her fill the tea urn for those wedding guests who could turn their mind to tea, my mother told me that as I was now eighteen I could stay over at Sean's. It was good to hear her call him 'Sean' rather than 'That Sean'. I kissed her hard on the cheek. I smelt her warm perfume and her hairspray keeping her hair just so. I left an imprint of my red lipstick on her cheek. We both laughed a bit too loudly as I rubbed at her cheek with a paper napkin, leaving a light blush on her skin. She told me to be careful, her eyes still shining with laughter. I could not look her squarely in the eye.

She did not know that we had already done it a million times; at his house, in the back of his car, under the apple trees, in the packing shed.

*

That night, he waited until I had unpacked my overnight bag, my bathrobe on top of his on the hook behind his bedroom door, my toothbrush in the glass beside his on the bathroom basin of his ensuite. He waited until we had ripped the purple taffeta bridesmaid dress I had worn that night. He waited until he had come in that tremulous, shut-eyed, silent way of his, before he told me that he was leaving in a week's time for Europe, for India, for South America, for wherever the fuck out of here.

I immediately said, 'Take me with you.'

The night after he left, when he was probably 33,000 feet above the earth, I sat on my bed and wrote words on my skin. I wrote extracts from Keats, I wrote his name, I wrote, 'Get me the fuck out of here.' The pen drew blood. I took thirty of my father's sleeping pills, which was just about the rudest thing I could have done in my parents' house; ruder than anything I managed to inscribe on my arm. I intended it to be the last night of my life. But of course it wasn't. I went into a coma for three days. No one told him what happened. 'This is just something that Sean has to do. He has to travel the world. Always has,' is how Mrs McIntyre explained it to me. I felt stunned at the mere sound of his name. My hands were sweating as they clutched the bunch of convalescence flowers she gave me, 'Gerberas,' she'd said, introducing them to me, and then she'd added brightly, 'Cheerful!' as if I was just sad. I found something I thought was pride and would not tell him in the short offended letters I sent for a time.

*

'Not much happened while you were gone,' I say quietly, laughing inwardly at the way we both define the last three years by his absence.

I wonder about Marianne and the last night of her life. Somehow, even if Sean were not here before me, I would have known he survived that accident.

'Where are you living now?' He leans, arms crossed, against the car. Even before I say it, I know that he wants to come with me wherever I am going. And I know that he probably will be coming with me, because not that much happened while he was gone.

Blind Date

Janette Turner Hospital

Though Peter, who is Lachlan's best friend, is incensed by the special arrangements for the wedding, Lachlan himself does not care. All that matters is what is going to happen when his father appears. There will be an organ fanfare. Everyone will stand. *Lachlan's father has come back,* the organ pipes will announce, and Lachlan will feel their low thunder through the soles of his feet. Outside there will be lightning and blinding rain, torrential and jubilant. Certainly the weather will change.

Lachlan believes he will know the moment his father steps inside the church. His father's particular way of walking will telegraph itself down the aisle, along the dark-stained floorboards, beneath the pew. Lachlan will decode the vibrations. This is something he has always been able to do. He reads footsteps.

Perhaps his father will speak to him in passing. Perhaps, as his father stands just behind the bride and groom, waiting for the minister to ask *Who giveth this woman ... ?*, perhaps he will turn to look at Lachlan and snap his fingers, the old sign. *G'day, mate,* he will murmur. *Long time, no see.*

Lachlan vividly remembers his father's voice: the smoky scratchy sound, soft at the edges, like a train going into a tunnel. He remembers the last words he heard his father say.

'I'm sorry, mate.' When his father said that, he was hugging Lachlan so tightly that all Lachlan could think of was *washing machine.* His face was pressed into his father's shirt where the collar met the yoke and there was a damp vibrating sweetness that Lachlan recognised. The smell was like baskets of clothing waiting to be ironed and like the mounds of sheet where his mother set him down while she folded and stacked. The sensation was familiar too: the sinking into softness, the smell of clean, the muted thrum against his ear.

When Lachlan's father shows up in dreams, he trails washdays.

Now, eight years later, Lachlan can distinguish the particular elements of bleach and washing powder and steam and fabric softener, a fragrance-cluster that triggers a furtive urge. On Mondays he still sneaks into the laundry room. He buries his face in hills of sheets as soft as ice-cream swirls. He curls up in the great laundry basket and hugs towels. He will never let anyone hear him or see him cry.

'I'm sorry, mate,' his father had said on that day, the day that he left. 'But I can't breathe.' There was a momentary faltering in his father's voice, the way a train whistle hesitates at the mouth of a tunnel. 'I'm drowning, mate, and I just can't breathe, that's all there is to it. I'm sorry.'

Lachlan has never told anyone, not even Peter, what his father said, but as the wedding draws close, he tries to tell his mother. 'Mum,' he says tentatively, 'you remember that day when Dad buggered off –'

'Lachlan!' She is folding laundry and she pauses with a pillowcase suspended in front of her, astonished. He knows that her eyebrows are raised. 'We don't use language like that in this household. What a dreadful expression. Where did you hear it?'

He almost says *From Pamela,* but stops in time. 'I heard someone say it yesterday,' he says.

'You know you're the reason that Dad buggered off, don't you?' his sister said. She is eleven years older than Lachlan. 'And would you please not spatter the mirror when you wash?

It's like a pigsty in here.'

Lachlan leaned over the bathroom sink. He felt sick. 'I didn't know,' he said.

'Sorry, Lockie. I know you don't know what a mess you make. I'm just jumpy. It's wedding jitters.'

'I didn't know about Dad.'

'Oh.' Pamela put a hand over her mouth. 'I shouldn't have said that. But why can't he just stay up there in Queensland and good riddance?'

The bathroom began to move like a swing. Lachlan groped for Pamela but stumbled and fell. 'You know where Dad is?' he whispered.

'Lockie, I can't hear you. Are you crying?'

'How do you know where Dad is?' he shouted.

Pamela looked startled. 'We've always known, Lockie. Here.' She helped him get up and led him to the wicker clothes hamper. 'Sit down.'

'Where is he?'

'Burdekin Dam, up in Queensland. That's what he wrote on the note he left Mum. *Gone to work on the Burdekin Dam. Fortune to be made,* blah blah blah. *We'll need plenty extra for Lachlan, I'll send back dosh for the special schools,* and then he just buggered off. Didn't fool anyone. You scared him, Lockie, that's the sad truth. He was running away from you.'

Lachlan slithered off the clothes hamper. He felt his way across the floor and curled up on the white tile beneath the wash basin and leaned his cheek against the chrome snake of pipe. Pamela reached down and pulled him out. 'Forget him, Lockie. He's a bloody coward and a shit and an idiot.'

'No!' Lachlan protested. 'That's not true.'

Pamela stroked his hair. 'We don't need him,' she said.

'And he did send money. Mum told me.'

'Blood money. Came from a lawyer, not from him. Not a word for eight years, not one letter, and now he wants to show up for my wedding. Talk about gall. If he *does* darken the church door, I'm going to turn right round in my wedding dress and tell him to bugger off.'

'Lachlan,' his mother says, 'is this the sort of thing you hear from Peter?'

'No,' Lachlan swears.

'Then where did you hear it?'

'I can't remember.' Lachlan has to be careful. He dreads his sister's rows with their mother. 'I didn't know it was bad,' he says, and that part is true. 'But Mum,' he persists – casually, cunningly – 'that day when Dad left, the day when the cyclone came –'

'What cyclone?' his mother says. 'There wasn't a cyclone.'

'Yes, there was,' Lachlan insists. He pulls at his fingers, one by one, and the knuckles give off small cracking sounds.

'Don't do that,' his mother says.

Lachlan keeps pulling at his fingers. He remembers his father setting him down on the verandah and walking into curtains of water. There was the washing day smell, the sound of waterfall, the sense of drowning. 'It rained and rained all day. It was dark like a thunderstorm.'

'For heaven's sake, Lachlan, you were two years old. You couldn't possibly remember what the weather was like and nor can I, for that matter, except I do know it wasn't raining because I had to walk down to the pub to find out why your father hadn't come home. I didn't find his note till the next day. So I had to walk half a mile and believe me, it wasn't raining.'

But Lachlan is sure that it was. And he does remember. He remembers water churning. He remembers deluge. He sees his father suspended in weeping, taking in air through his gills. Last year, on the news, Lachlan heard about a man and a boy in a rubber boat when a cyclone hit. *Tossed like matchsticks in foam,* the newscaster said, *both of them drowned,* and Lachlan's mother had to call the doctor because her son had turned blue in the face.

'It was pouring,' Lachlan whispers. 'It was a cyclone. Dad had to swim for his life.'

'Lockie, we don't get cyclones in Melbourne,' his mother says. 'You're seeing things again.' She feels his forehead. 'You're running a temperature.' She smooths the stacked sheets. She leans over and kisses Lachlan on the top of his head. 'I know you're worried, Lachlan, we all are, but he'll probably chicken out. He probably won't even show up. That's what he's like.'

Lachlan can hear a roaring in his ears. There are rocks and spray and everything is green and dark and he is floundering and then everything is black.

*

'He's seeing things again,' he hears his mother tell Pamela.

Pamela puts her face on the pillow next to his. She strokes his cheek. 'We won't even let him inside the church,' she whispers. 'I promise. He's such a shit.'

Lachlan turns his face to the wall.

Pamela says brightly: 'Look, I've got something to show you.'

She puts a white satin cushion on the bed and reaches for his hand. She runs his fingers over the cushion. She lets him feel the heavy ivory lace along each edge. 'It's the ring-bearer's cushion,' she says. 'Do you like it?'

'Yes.' Lachlan strokes the satin. 'It's beautiful.' He explores the lace with his fingertips.

'And here's your suit for the wedding.'

Lachlan trails his fingers across the satin vest, the bow-tie, the pin-tucked shirt of finest cotton.

'You are going to look magnificent,' his mother says.

My father will be proud, Lachlan thinks.

'The vest and the bow-tie are teal blue,' Pamela tells him. 'Same as the flower-girl's dress and the bridesmaids' gowns.'

Lachlan imagines teal blue. *Teal.* It is a strange and beautiful word. He thinks of roses swaying underwater. He loves to press the petals against his lips. He loves the smell.

'What can you see?' Pamela asks.

'Teal roses,' Lachlan says, 'that grow underwater.'

Pamela laughs. 'Can you see I'm happy?' she asks.

'Yes,' Lachlan says. 'There's pink sugar all over your heart.'

'That's not pink sugar, that's Rodney,' she says.

*

Pamela met Rodney – who is Peter's uncle – on a blind date that was arranged by Peter's parents. In another week, she will marry Rodney. For the wedding, Lachlan is the ring-bearer, but it has been decided that he should not process down the aisle with the bridal party for fear he might step on his sister's train or jostle his little cousin Libby in her frothy flower-girl skirt. Libby's mother, in particular, thinks that Lachlan's presence in the processional would be 'unwise' and that 'special arrangements' should be made.

Peter is incensed by these special arrangements. He finds them insulting. He believes they have both been insulted, he and Lachlan. 'Anyway,' he says, 'Libby's so *icky,* she'd probably bump into *you.* I bet she wears socks with lace edges. I bet she wears lolly-pink panties with stupid little rosebuds stitched on.'

'She's OK,' Lachlan says. 'It's not her fault. Her dress is going to be teal blue. It matches my vest and bow-tie.'

'You have to make them understand,' Peter insists. 'You can't let people treat us like this.'

A lot of things make Peter rage and fume. Lachlan wonders why he himself is never angry. He supposes he must be too busy being sad. He does not know if this is a good thing or a bad thing, but he does know that he and Peter are lucky to have each other. They are going to be related. Second cousins by marriage, his mother says. They go to the same school, a special school, a boarding school in one of Melbourne's leafiest suburbs – *Snob hill,* Pamela calls it, *but you better not get a swelled head, Lockie, or I'll put ice in your pillow* – and every weekend they go home. Sometimes they both spend the weekend at Peter's house, which is in Carlton, and sometimes they both stay at Lachlan's, and sometimes each is alone with his family. Lachlan's favourite weekends are at Peter's house, but he feels guilty about this. His mother's sorrow presses down on him like a pillow over his face.

Once, for her birthday, he stole a rose from somebody's garden and gave it to her, and she burst into tears and went to her bedroom and closed the door. Lachlan climbed into the plum tree in the back yard until Pamela cajoled him down. 'Birthdays are difficult for Mum,' she explained. 'And it's kind of weird, what you did, because Dad used to give her a birthday rose.' She laughed. 'You must have got the rose-giving gene. How did you find it?'

'I smelled it. It was sticking through Mrs. Watt's fence.'

'Dad probably stole them, too.'

'Is that why Mum didn't like it?'

'You're too much like Dad, Lockie.'

'But I didn't really steal it. It was sticking through. It was outside her property. I just wanted to make Mum happy. I thought she'd like it.'

'She did like it, Lockie, she loved it, but it made her miss Dad. Or made her mad at him all over again, or something.' Pamela sighed. She held her little brother away from her, studying him. 'Mum and me both think you're the bee's knees, so don't ever forget that. But see, you weren't supposed to happen. You came as a big surprise and it kind of messed things up between Mum and Dad. And then, you know, when you gave them the *second* surprise … '

*

'So, Lachlan, your dad's coming down from Queensland for the wedding,' Peter's father says. 'It'll be good to see him again.'

Lachlan pulls at his fingers. 'How do you know my dad?' he asks.

'Same way we know your mum,' Peter's mother says. 'We met at the school when you and Peter were just babies.'

'My dad buggered off,' Lachlan says. 'Because of me.'

'Who the hell told you that?'

'Pamela told me.'

'Well, it's not true,' Peter's dad says.

'Partly, maybe,' Peter's mother says.

'There were a whole lot of reasons. As a matter of fact, your father took off with another woman.'

'For God's sake, Benjamin!' Peter's mother says.

'He's going to hear about it sooner or later, from someone. These things happen, Lachlan. Your mum and your dad: they're both terrific, but they didn't really get on, and your dad was having an affair long before you came on the scene. It was a bit of a mess all round, but these things happen. He's a good bloke, your dad.'

'A ladies' man,' Peter's mother says. 'A real charmer.'

'You're his spitting image,' Peter's dad says.

'By now, he's cheating on Judy,' Peter's mother says. 'I'd be willing to bet on that.'

*

Lachlan has many conversations with his father. There is always floodwater rising. They are always swimming for their lives.

How come you never even send me birthday cards? Lachlan asks him.

My new wife won't let me, his father says. *She's jealous.*

But sometimes his father says: *I do send you birthday cards, but your mum hides them. She's still mad at me.*

Pamela's mad at you too, Lachlan tells him.

Are you mad at me?

No, Lachlan says. *Sometimes. Do you miss me?*

Every single day, his father says. Sometimes he says that. Sometimes he says: *Who are you?*

Sometimes Lachlan's father is in a military line-up of deserters. *Which one is he?* the general demands, and Lachlan moves from one manacled prisoner to the next. One man smells of football games, another of grass cuttings. Lachlan smells fabric softener and bleach. *This man is my father,* he says.

Fire! the general orders, and Lachlan hurls himself in front of the condemned man and dies a hero.

My son, my son, his father sobs.

Sometimes Lachlan's picture is on the front page of every newspaper because he has invented a new kind of Braille. *This is how it works,* he explains on television. He is sitting in front of his computer. *When your fingers touch a word on the keyboard,* he says, *pictures open in your brain like buds opening. You can see what you read and what you write.*

The TV producer interrupts. *Excuse me,* he says, *but we've just had a call come in from your father. He's watching the show.*

I know, Lachlan says. *I can see him.*

*

'It's Wagner,' Peter whispers. 'It's from Lohengrin.'

'I know that. We're 'sposed to turn round now.'

'Shh,' Lachlan's mother warns.

They are in the front pew, and Lachlan is balancing the ring-bearer's cushion on his upturned palms. The two rings are tethered to satin loops. Lachlan, Peter and Lachlan's mother all turn to face the open church doors, and Lachlan can feel the blinding sun warm against his eyes, he can actually see it, really see it, a dazzle of gold and white. He has always been able to tell light from dark. From somewhere in the heart of the radiance, Pamela is coming toward them, her lace train and her flower-girl and her bridesmaids behind her. When Pamela approaches the front pew, she is going to reach for Lachlan's right hand, and he will hold the ring-bearing cushion against his chest with his left hand and go up with his sister to stand in front of the minister, where Rodney is already waiting. Lachlan's mother will also step forward. When the minister asks *Who giveth this woman … ?* Lachlan's mother will say: *I do.*

'Mum,' Lachlan whispers. 'Did he come?'

'She looks so lovely,' his mother says, with a break in her voice. Lachlan knows she is crying.

Peter tugs at the back of Lachlan's vest. 'Someone's pushing me,' he murmurs. 'I think it's him.'

Lachlan can feel a man's hand on his shoulder. Floodwaters press him. He is floundering. He goes over the lip of the falls. Pamela touches his wrist. He is drowning in happiness.

'Dad!' Pamela says. 'You've got a nerve.'

'You look gorgeous,' her father says.

'I should tell you to bugger off, Dad.'

'Please,' the minister says.

'You look good too, Elly.'

'You too, Jim,' Lachlan's mother says. 'You should be shot just the same.'

'Probably.'

Lachlan tugs at his father's sleeve. 'I'm Lachlan,' he says.

'*Who giveth this woman … ?*' the minister asks.

Lachlan's father scoops up his son in a bear hug and the ring cushion rises like a snowbird in flight and hovers over Pamela and falls. It hits Rodney softly on the head.

'*Who giveth this woman … ?*' the minister repeats.

'Do you remember me?' Lachlan whispers.

'I do,' his father says. 'I do.'

Certain Things I'd Say About Girls

Graeme Kinross-Smith

' … what a lovely way to burn … '
(from 'Fever' – Davenport/Cooley)

CLOSED FOR BUSINESS? – When I was at school I knew a girl I wanted to taste as urgently as chocolate – her eyelashes, her water-bubbler laugh – but she seemed to be closed for business even when she looked my way. It was as if she looked right past me. She held onto the handrails, advanced a leg, and dipped her toe in the waiting swimming pool like a deer. Then she looked past me again. I should have known, but I didn't know much in those days.

TOTTING UP USEFULNESS – Another girl I knew in my school years used to smile at me like a real estate agent as we talked sitting on the hot brick steps on the way home from the Baths. But I could tell when she inspected her calves, when she turned her thighs in her short shorts to peer at them, that she was totting up my usefulness and how much her brother might have told me. Her brother had told me plenty. His sister was a bloody Mother Superior, he said. His sister was a pain. And she flirted with the boys from the private school. Even so, I dreamt about her pale thighs.

PURITY – Then there was the girl smell and girl purity. In their tunics they smelled like those tasteless strawberry wafers. They were faultless. Their eyes were different – they were like secret little lakes you come on unsuspecting in the forest. And there were the looks they flashed – girls, I concluded, could probably dive into mirrors and disappear. Or they could incinerate me on the spot with a single glance.

AFTERWARDS – NO TRAMS – Girls put you down. Girls put you in your place. The first girl I kissed had beautiful breasts, but she couldn't help intimidating me. After the kiss, as we stood breathless at her door, she squirmed away from me and said that it was mmm ... OK. Only OK? How the hell were you supposed to do it? I walked all the way home afterwards, sniffing the privet hedges in the dark streets, wondering, empty. That late, the last tram had gone anyway.

THE DISTANCE BETWEEN CITIES – One time, after my marriage break-up, I drove 850 km to see another beautiful girl I'd got to know – without saying I was coming. She was in bed reading by the time I came to a stop in front of her garage. It was late. She let me in, shaking her head, her face pale with surprise, and when I'd had a wash and cleaned my teeth and slipped into the sheets beside her she insisted I lie straight for a while like a log until she had adjusted to having me in her bed. I lay there, hearing the quiet stroking of the travelling clock on the dressing-table near the bed. It was the clock that accompanied her life. I felt an intruder. Minutes passed. Who was I to be here, to spring this surprise? What had I been thinking of? And my eyes felt tired and dazzled by the headlights on the highway. And then she let me worm my hand under her shoulder and take her in my arms. So we lay and talked and started to plan what we could do the following day. It was a Saturday, and a long weekend. Just when she was thinking aloud again about me being there – 'you, here!' – she unravelled herself, sat up, and in one movement pulled her nightie over her head and threw it over the chair. Ah, a beautiful girl, I said. We both remained beautiful people for each other for another five months, whenever we could get together. Then the arguments over who should come to whom began to dig deep. Then the surprise was gone. It got to be hard work. The distance between cities beat us.

TO MOVE IT ABOUT – Another friend of mine, Jack, tells me a strange / sad / uplifting story of a mate of his, Stewart, whose friendship dates from their earlier years, from his time at school and at university in Brisbane. Jack recalls dark, dapper Stewart as always being undemonstrative and retiring, striding emotionless and uncommitted beside his harem-scarem friends and the hoitem-toitem girls as they swam in closer and closer circles around each other in the later years at high school and then across the green sward and sandstone of the university. It was behaviour that worried and intrigued Jack, who on his own admission was a wanton wastrel during those years and up for anything, including a fling now and then with this girl and that. Did Stewart feel nothing in the presence of these breathing, beautiful fillies, Jack asked himself? Apparently not. He seemed to be quite unstirred. Jack looked at him. Perhaps Stewart knew nothing! So, one hot weekend at university, to the sound of thongs sticking and unsticking along the humid lino of the college corridors, Jack set up Stewart for an evening with Jill of the entreating, generous eyes and the tanned, full shoulders and alluring cleavage. Everyone liked Jill. Why didn't Stewart, Jack suggested to his mate, shout Jill dinner on Saturday night to celebrate the submission of her thesis – in that softly lit restaurant, say, buried just a few streets away in St Lucia? They were both psychology students, after all, both battling the same assessment demons, so to speak. Stewart said yes, maybe he would, yes. Yes – good idea. He'd tee it up. And afterwards, Jack hastened to suggest secretly to Jill – who had more than once put herself in the way of Stew's dark-haired and understated charm to no avail, who had herself puzzled to Jack about Stew's asexual, shy serenity – that she might work on Stewart after dinner, might entice him to a night in her college room in the name of research – and they'd see where it went from there.

Afterwards … Monday morning in fact … Jack checked. Yes, Stewart said wryly, his face warning that he did not want to be drawn, but yes, he and Jill had gone out for dinner. Nothing more? Oh, well, yes … he … yes, well … they … er … they'd stayed … he'd ended up staying the night with Jill. Stewart gave a brief smirk of surprise at his own admission, then quickly covered it. And how was it? Well, it was OK. Jill's nice. And sex? Ah, well, yes, we played around a bit … it was hot, you know. And … ? And what? Was it good? Ah, it was OK. It was OK. I like Jill a lot. Stewart's brow was furrowing. Yair, but she seemed very quiet. She was nice, but she just seemed to be waiting … Jill was really nice. Stewart looked a bit desolate. You had an erection, yes? Jack bored in. You penetrated, yes? Yes. What happened? Well, nothing much. Jack was puzzled. You moved around a bit, didn't you? You didn't lie like a log? You moved it about a bit?? Sensation! You know, Jack said, movement and sensation for you both. Like when you jack off. Rubbing it up and down, pleasuring her? She liked it? It's better than jacking off, isn't it? There was a pause. Stewart looked away. Then he looked Jack in the eye. Then he looked away again. I've never jacked off, he said. Never ever done it.

Now, all these years later, Jack stops in the telling of the story. His cheeks, his eyes, look as though they'll explode with amused disbelief. Never jacked off in his life! And do you know, he says, after not seeing Stew now for fifteen years – the occasional letter, an email now and then: he's been living in the States for years now – we're going over, Eugenie and I, to his wedding! Can't believe it! Denver in the Fall! And that's not all. Do you know what he does over there, with his psychology Masters? He's a relationship counsellor. A marriage guidance counsellor! A field where an intimate understanding of how girls tick, what turns them on and off, might seem to be a prerequisite, wouldn't you think! He's come a long way, our Stew. And here he is – marrying another psychologist at the age of thirty-seven. It'll be great to see him. I think our Stew's come a long, long way!

LOVE AND THE AXE – The third girl I ever made love to had never watched anyone use an axe. The morning after the night before I was stashing the axe in the back of the truck to go and get a bit more firewood and she said she wanted to come with me into the bush. I was pleased. She was beautiful. She watched me work. She watched the axe blade bite into the wet log one way, then the other. She watched the chips fly. She watched the scarf deepen, first from one side, then the other. The trees murmured above us in the autumn wind, waiting for winter. She could see how I love using an axe, have always loved it. Is that how it's done, she said. That night when the moon had left the deep window and the room was black she came to me again under the doona, her mouth probing, finding me, working up my thighs, and then her teeth and tongue teasing my foreskin. I lay back in precious agony. My lips blessed her as she played. I stroked her hair, her forehead. In the morning, over muesli, over toast, she asked me questions. Could we get in some more firewood? And where did I get the axe? Garage sale, I said. Lucky! The bloke selling it didn't know what he had. It's a beautiful axe, I said. Perfect balance. It's a Sater. It's Swedish. I don't know whether they make them any more. A Sater, she said. A Sater. A Sater? And she rolled it around in her mouth and on her breath. I should have married her, but I didn't. Instead, four years later, I married my wife – and look where that got me.

STARTING OVER – 'At least I've preserved my marriage, which is more than you can say!' She was spitting it at me. This was my best friend's wife, who had never had any time for me. She was a girl – a girl I'd known for some time, you might say – but she couldn't stand me. I knew it was wisest to shrug. My best friend was ready. He stepped in like a batsman to deflect his wife's words, her pout, her blazing eyes. 'Cricket's the thing,' my best friend said. 'Cricket is indeed the thing! We'd better get going. The Third Test beckons.' And we headed off in my best friend's Falcon. Halfway to the SCG, his eyes still searching for gaps in the traffic as he drove, my best friend cleared his throat and asked: 'And how're you getting on? Separation and so on?' So I sat back in the seat and thought about how I was getting on for a few moments. Then I said: 'Oh, I'll make it in the end. But it's bloody lonely. Suddenly no kids: I really miss them. No household to come home to. And it's slow. You have to start all over again. Starting over – at my age! Wasted years! That's how it feels. A waste!' The traffic was slowing around us, coming up to the lights. Cars slotted themselves into new lanes. My best friend pulled up carefully, close to the Charade in front. He glanced away out the driver's window, then dragged in a huge breath. He turned to look at me: 'I'd give anything – and I mean anything! – to be able to start all over again.' His voice rang in the car. His arms were like ramrods gripping the wheel, ready to wrench it from the steering column.

THE CONTINUUM – Girls are girls, I conclude. That girl! These girls! I stare at the word. I love it. Girls. I devour the five letters. Sometimes I savour the sound of the word so long in my mind and in my mouth that the letters begin to make something else, to mean something else. The word repeats. The word dissolves the years. We are forever young. The word opens a prospect of orange ripeness against which I see beautiful eyes. The word ushers in husky voices and eyelashes. It opens the door to scents that wring my heart. Girls are mango and apple juice together. They are the scent of mandarin blossom in the sun. I remember even the subtle musk smell of my former wife. The short word opens a long, light-filled hall of sounds. The girl who I love now is a cello – her dignified belly, her soft, thoughtful sentences, her contralto laugh. Or she could be an opera singer, the way her words come to me like Jessie Norman's. She looks at me over the plates she is setting out. She makes a gentle display, smiling for me, her mouth opening, her eyebrows raised, her hands spreading, her eyes reaching for me with challenging love. The kitchen and the dining table settle around us in the soft gloom. Outside the window the late-in-the-day light of a weekend floods through the trees from the west. We know without looking that the sun's tableau is there, how rich and sad it is. It drenches us both with a certainty. We step closer, our hands touch. We reach for each other – lips, hair, shoulders, breasts, thighs, calves, twining feet and ankles. It is a close clasping. We teeter, because we know and yet we don't know. There is more to go. There is more to unveil. There is skin to touch again and again. We kiss. Our lips know each other. We clasp. We are juices, mingling. She folds inside me, I fold inside her, against the days we can hear coming.

Wild Horses

Joanna Kujawa

She wanted to be alone in Bali. In her dreams she saw herself in free sail, arms spread to the good winds blowing through the islands east of Java. East of Java – this phrase has a special meaning in her first language where *jawa* means 'waking'. Strange geography of words.

East of waking then, she sailed with her arms spread to the dreamy islands of the long Indonesian archipelago. Geographically speaking, Bali is the first of small islands off Java's coast, followed by Lombok and the string of other islands that like pearls spread further east to Irian Jaya. North of Bali is the huge circle of Borneo with memories of white rajas and Conrad. South of Bali is the great Indian Ocean reaching out to Australia.

She wanted to be alone in Bali. In free sail with the good winds ... She did not ask him to come. She did not want anyone to come. Her romance with Bali was not supposed to be changed to a romance in Bali. She needed space. She announced it to the world. In a loud voice of a woman who had finally found herself. Who decided to celebrate her Self.

But now she waits for an Australian man at the tiny airport in Denpasar, the man she hardly knows, the man with whom she has had the briefest of affairs in another place, in another time. Now she can't help but want him to come. Otherwise she would feel cheated.

This is how it is.

The man arrives. Qantas flight 29. From Melbourne via Sydney.

Two hours earlier she rented a cottage in Ubud. A piece of paradise bought at a small price. It was the first place she visited and she has rented it without doing what she should have done – bargain for a better price. The place is not a place. It is a miniature Hindu temple, with a great porch in a garden, among flowers and lovebirds hung in delicate and ornate cages under the roofs of cottages. The carvings on that temple show Hindu gods feasting on love, in erotic poses, symbols of their creative urge. *The world would not exist. The luscious gardens would not exist. The birds of paradise would not exist. The sensuous beauty of the world would not exist if it were not for us,* they say. *If it were not for our divine lust. Lust for Creation.* With that knowledge she looks at the bed which faces a terrace opened to another cascading garden and more temples and more ancient gods making love and more flowers and birds and colours … Lost in their own beauty.

It rains in the afternoon.

They sit on the terrace. A long, long bamboo leans towards them with heavy raindrops on its elegant leaves, outlining itself in sharp lines, like a Japanese print, against the luscious greenery of the garden.

The man pours some vodka into a teapot and mixes it with sweet orange Fanta. Disgusting.

They laugh.

They drink it as if it were a soft drink; the killer vodka and the sickening sweet drink. Two things that should not be together but somehow are perfect. Together. This kind of thing happens all the time, they think, but no one says it because it would piss off the order of the society.

The tyrant, they agree, the society is the tyrant. He laughs and pours her more vodka and more sweet orange into the little teacup that she holds in her hand.

'You have the most beautiful wrists,' he says.

She is amazed. Amazed that the man, overwhelmed by desire, kisses her wrists, but does not notice her *other* beauty that *other* men praise. He sees her differently, he says. He sees what others don't see. He sees her soul in her slim wrists. His heart lives now in her wrists. Dreams about her wrists. Doesn't want anyone else to touch her wrists. They are his.

He gets up, pulls her towards him and they dance to Iggy Pop coupled up in a French ballad with Françoise Hardy: a wild punk and a French siren of cafés – another couple that should not work but does.

So they, too, do the wild thing together that they will never forget.

'Never?'

Never. What do you think you will remember on your deathbed? That you paid off the mortgage? That you left money in the bank or renovated a house? No, you will remember this. All the unpredictable, wonderful things in life that you did and felt guilty about. The more beautiful ways of being.

Hmmm. Maybe she is right. She quotes poets. She quotes mystics. As she lies naked next to him.

Live free. Fear is the only shadow that stops you from salvation. A masterful device of your private demons who want you in your own chains. Stewed in your own private soup. Do you think that you see heaven when you die? No, you see exactly what you created here. A life. Lost in the labyrinth of guilt. That's your original sin. The fear. The guilt. That thing that stops you from opening to fulfilment. Or life that whispers the promises of great beauty to you. But only if you open to the unknown.

He breathes caressing words into her ear as he eats it away, kisses it when they dance on this terrace overlooking the luscious gardens of Ubud.

He brought some tapes with him. To share his music with her. Patti Smith. *The Horses.*

She listens to him. She listens to the music, feels vodka's

maddening courage and hears the wild woman screaming, 'Horses! Horses!' She pushes him inside the cottage, into the bed of the Hindu gods, onto his back. She sits on him sideways as if he were her horse and she his crazy rider and she dances on top of him, like that, screaming together with him and with Patti, 'Suddenly! Horses! Possibilities!'

They fall exhausted. Suddenly tender. With the inexhaustible tenderness that neither of them has known until this moment. All masks fall down. All pretence. In this moment is the sweetest lust for creation. The desire for beauty that they see in each other.

Suddenly. The intensity of merging. Two become one. Oneness. Riding like wild horses ... without attachments ... without a past to haunt them ... without a future to tempt them ... In this moment they ride into the light. Feel no fear. No separateness. Suddenly everything is holy. Everything. The glimpse of it. Seen through desire.

He kisses her.

He can feel her breath at his neck. On his face. His penis inside her. So warm, so wet. His body heavy on her. A sweet and overwhelming sensation that she gives him. The foreignness of her body, so different from that body he is used to. He traces his fingers on the curve of her breast. A different curve altogether. A warmth that the other body has lost for him. That other, more familiar body. The labyrinth. The net of the things from the Past.

'I'd love to have met you when you were seventeen,' he touches her with his fingers as she opens for him. 'Already sexy but still untouched. You would've been my slave. I would've lied to you and you would've believed me because you wouldn't have known better. I would have been a father to your children.'

'You already have children,' she says. 'I don't want to be a slave. I want to be free with you.'

'Free with me?' His fingers stop and he looks at her. 'That doesn't exist. That freedom together is called bondage.'

She doesn't believe him. She looks deceivingly sweet to him.

Her long hair falls all over her face like a veil. And she doesn't believe him even more.

'You are a coward. You are a prissy little coward,' she says and she kisses him on the chin.

The first time they made love was in Kuala Lumpur where she was working at the time. He came to her apartment and said how much he would miss her. Three days since he had seen her in a red *cheong sum* imprinted with black butterflies. With a sweet smell of perfume that he did not know. They kissed.

'Can I come back after dinner?' he asked. 'I will read you my favourite poems by Robert McAlmon.' McAlmon, the poet who was in Paris with Hemingway, Fitzgerald and Stein. He felt for him because he died unhappy and disillusioned.

He had such an interesting life, she thinks. Why do we need to be appreciated by others to be happy?

After dinner they read the poems. Then she watched him stripping off his clothes, the steel-coloured shirt and the dark-grey pants, showing her his muscular body. Her eyes caressing his strong thighs, his penis well-shaped and erect, the shy grace of his movements as he walked towards her. She let him in without a condom. Slowly. Gently. Something she never does.

To feel him deeply.

Fully. Connected. Merged.

If there is one thing wrong with Bali, the *Lonely Planet* says, it is the ugly, vicious, Balinese dogs. They are ugly, alright. Ugly, poor devils. And they bark constantly. It bothers him. The constant barking of the ugly dogs. In the middle of the night he gets up, opens the door of the cottage to the serene Balinese sky and howls at them, 'Shut up! Fuck! Shut up! You sons of the bitches!'

'Why are you so angry?' she asks him when he is back in bed.

He has been angry since his father died when he was eleven, he tells her. Since they became so poor that people brought them food for Christmas out of pity. He hated everything. He hated the poverty. He hated the pity. He felt powerless at the servility of his mother. He felt powerless after his father's death. So powerless! Powerless. Powerless ...

He sobs. Her arms wrap protectively around him.

That's why he will not leave his wife and his boys. He can't leave his wife because he would be penniless. And he can't leave because he wants his boys to have a better childhood than he had. That's why he will stay at his day job and will not write the movies he wants to write. For the money. To give them the security that he has never had.

She lets go. Her arms around her knees now.

'I love the reasons why people stay together,' she says defiantly. 'They enhance my sense of romance.'

One afternoon, a small man wanders into the garden. He seems completely displaced in this paradise of orange birds, yellow hibiscus, purple and violet orchids and the ever-present, eye-blinding intensity of bougainvilleas. His head is shaped like a dead coconut, his hands resemble the legs of an old and tired octopus. He carries a roll of papers under his arm and smiles like a child when she notices him. She looks like an insolent, foreign princess to him, sitting high on the porch, sipping her tea and listening to the song of a lovebird in a cage. Hesitant and shy, he circles around her several times, his baby smile fixed on his ancient face. He circles around the verandah like a scared bird, trying to figure out whether she is a hunter or a friend. Finally he bows and asks if he can show her something.

'Sure.'

The little coconut man unwraps the scrolls with great care.

'These are my drawings and paintings,' he says, lowering his eyes.

He shows her one painting after another unsure of her judgement. 'This is what I do when I have time. This is for me. Joy for me.' He says, very quietly.

'What are you doing when you don't paint?'

'I work for food.'

'What do you do for food?'

The little man smiles shyly, 'I work in rice fields. This,' he points to his paintings, 'doesn't bring food. This is love.'

'Ah,' she understands.

She picks a drawing of a dancer and the little man disappears from her life.

Back to the rice fields. For food.

At night, they go to a restaurant, eat pasta and listen to *Degung Sabilungan* music, the soft tones of Balinese gamelan sounds fill the night. She drinks too much. He is guilt-ridden. He is afraid. What if his wife will not let him back into the house. She was furious with him for leaving her in the middle of renovations and going to Bali. He will have to explain himself. It will be tough. What if he says 'we' instead of 'I'. She will take all the money, she said so and he does not want to be poor ever again. Never again to be poor. You don't understand, he tells her, how awful it is to be poor and alone. He does not want to be there, in that situation again, when he is an old man of forty-three.

Forty-three is not old, she tells him but he does not believe her. He feels old. He leaves her in the restaurant and runs to the closest cyber café to send a message to his wife that he's got terrible tonsillitis, has an outrageous fever and generally is not enjoying himself. Then he buys a bracelet for his wife. Will pass for silver. He has to lie, he explains, if he wants to be admitted back into his house.

He never calls his wife by name. As if he does not want to wake up a ghost. Ah, it is a long story. Of love. Of responsibilities. Of lost souls who cannot save each other anymore. Two souls who share the memories of the past that is deadening them. Of powerful silences. And lies.

She didn't invite this man here. Before, she was always free. Before, her heart was always free. How has this man invaded her life and made her a captive?

'You evil seductress.' He caresses her knee under the table. 'I can smell you. Let's go back to the cottage, you feline woman.'

So she drinks more. On the way to the cottage, she falls into a three-foot deep sewer. One can't see anything at night, the streets are not lit.

'Jesus Christ! Are you OK?'

He finds only a small cut as he inspects her legs. No disinfectant around. He cleans the cut with bottled water and pours the rest of the vodka on it. He licks her knee, presses his head against her thighs and they fly again like the newly married from Chagall's paintings.

In the morning, over his peppermint tea, he tells Lawrence how she almost broke her leg last night. Lawrence is the lovebird who lives in a cage under the roof of our verandah and speaks many tongues.

Towards the end, he really gets sick. In Jimbaran, a small fishing village, ten minutes from the airport by taxi. It was their next hideaway after Ubud. His friend had told him it was a great place and he wanted to see a beach in Bali. Just across from the beach, in a small hotel, he gets his tonsillitis.

'It is psychosomatic,' she tells him. 'So no one would believe that you had a good time here.'

Now, she is angry with him. Furious. Fire raging in her belly. She believes, no!, she *knows* that he has made himself sick so he could later pretend this magic did not happen. He will lie so much about this trip until he himself will believe it was a disaster and he was sick all the time.

She goes for a walk on the beach until she reaches a meeting point for the fishermen. Amazing that such a place still exists in Bali. Hardly any foreigners. Fishermen smile at her but let her be and continue with their tasks. She watches them pulling their narrow, Viking-like boats towards the sea. She watches them jumping into their boats in their colourful sarongs, joking with each other. Laughing. Surrounded by children, the women sit on the sand. Black, silky hair; dark, bright eyes. Old women dig in the sand for small oysters. Chatty like the sea which comes to the beach and retreats again, day after day. Everything is the sea here. Everything is the fish. People smell of the sea and of the fish. The air smells of the sea and of the fish. And the kites! She nearly missed the kites. The kites are high in the sky. Like magical airplanes or persistent Balinese gods watching over humans with amusement.

When she comes back to the hotel he has a high fever.

He does not have any money left. She calls for a doctor. A small, scared woman doctor comes in with an even smaller male nurse. She explains the problem to her. She lies as he would lie, that he was sick all week and needs a 'certificate', 'something official' to prove it. The tiny doctor smiles knowingly.

'It will cost.'

'How much?'

'Thirty Australian dollars.'

'No, Jo, no. We have no money,' he mumbles in fever.

She gives the shrewd doctor the money. The doctor looks at her, 'How long was your friend sick? Two weeks?'

'No, no. One week is enough.'

'One week then.' The doctor back-dates the certificate, signs it and hands it to her. She throws it at him. The doctor smiles and leaves.

On the last night they walk on the back streets of Jimbaran, the village they didn't see, away from the beach and the sea. Small, hidden streets behind a thousand-year-old Hindu temple, decorated with offerings to the gods. Rice, flowers and fruit on tiny trays of palm leaves. The statues of gods in checkered sarongs around their hips and blood-red hibiscus flowers behind their elongated ears. Their stone bodies are overgrown with the moss of the monsoon tropics. Old men gambling, betting on the upcoming cock fights, checking out the red and yellow roosters, caressing their magnificent, rainbow-like tails. Old women sitting in front of their houses, toothless but content, smiling, saying, 'Hello' to the two pale foreigners who walk where they shouldn't, picking at their private lives.

'Why did you leave your husband, Jo?'

She didn't leave her husband, she tells him. She left the whole life around him. She left ten years. She left a life. One life of many other possible lives.

She leaves the street, the sweet incense-smelling street, and walks toward the beach.

The sea and the sky are dark with the night. She can't really see any stars because of the smoke from the restaurants on the beach – smoked fish, grilled fish, beer, *arak* ... The smells mix with the salty sea and the quiet, foggy night without visible stars but they are somewhere up there, above them. She likes the darkness ahead of them. The darkness as a disguised light. The uncertainty. The possibilities hovering somewhere there in the unknown. The possibilities. Horses galloping through her head. Wild horses. Seahorses. The sea of possibilities. She walks into the sea. In free sail, arms spread to the good winds. *Jawa.* Bali. East of waking. The water is warm and the waves are whispery, they tell secrets at that time of the night. So many secrets, so many questions without answers.

Love and lust are wild horses galloping ... *Wild horses, fire in the heart, where are you taking us?* Love ... Seen through desire.

He touches her arm.

'Where are you going, Jo?'

'Just going.'

'Where?'

'Just going.'

'Just going,' he repeats softly and looks at her even softer as if he were going to cry. 'Just going, Jo?'

This Thistle

Chris Mansell

This thistle is in the garden of my good friend Annie. She says she is growing it to see how it will turn out. I don't know what she expects but there is a Scotch thistle in her front garden now which is taller than she is, and taller even than her rangy lover, Jill.

Jill slopes through the garden as if there were creatures to be hunted. She carries her shoulders high, as if she is balancing a spear in her right hand, her left ready to be stretched out in front of her, any minute, for balance. Actually, she always walks this way, even if it is in the mall nearby – a palatial, airconditioned temple to intimidation. Jill is not intimidated in these places. She carries her invisible spear always. Annie is more accommodating of the world, or perhaps less vigilant. She sees the thistle as a beautiful experiment and takes her cup of tea into the garden so that she can watch this outrageous thistle grow. Jill does not join her today. She is out looking for white paint and new tools because she moved in to Annie's shadowy house and is plotting further openness, light and space. The dark rooms make Jill anxious and fretful, although she cannot say why.

Annie is sitting in the front garden with her cup of pure tea thinking about nothing but the thistle all morning. Being able to concentrate is one of her strengths. Eventually, however, she will have to get up and take her gentle body into the house and begin again to do those things that she must do to stay alive: work, cook, eat, clean. It is not so much a burden now that her children have moved away. There is not so much to do, not so much to clean, and the fights and the crying have diminished and changed themselves into occasional visits. These days she likes how the shining floorboards make life seem simple and easily accomplished. Jill stalks around the offspring when they visit, issuing praise and handing out awkward squares of kindness as best she can.

There had been little discussion when Jill moved in. It seemed natural. Annie remembered the first time they'd met: Jill's shoulders had become stiffer, her alertness sharpened – but at the time Annie was already defeated by everything around her and Jill put down the spear for a moment and was calm and angular and Annie had had to accept.

When the thistle was two metres high, Jill decided that it was time for it to go. It was early evening and Annie was not yet home. The air was soft and temperate and fitted Jill as if it were made for her. The light breathed gently and each plant in the garden seemed to be an individual and have a definable identity. Life force she said to herself, though she didn't believe it. It was something Annie would say. She went to the kitchen and found a knife – she imagined that it would need cutting down; she imagined its fibrous stem would be tough and unsnappable. When she stood in front of it though, it was taller than she was, its purple flower nodded down, and suddenly it seemed too personal a violation to take the knife to it. She put the weapon down and considered this thing, its height and threat.

She knew it was a thistle, so by definition spiky, but she had assumed the long wide leaves were for show and not a promise of violence. She was wrong. The leaves were armed with spines, the stem decorated with an abrasive frill. She searched for a way in: a way to grasp the creature without doing damage to herself. She had to retreat.

She sat on the step and planned her next assault more carefully. This thistle was not going to surrender. Jill got sunglasses to protect her eyes, an old sweater, garden gloves, a spade, and a large fork she'd used to break up the ground for the vegetable beds out the back.

She advanced and loosened the surrounding soil with the fork, digging the tines deep and allowing air and light into the secret earth.

Then she put her hands around its body and hefted it backwards expecting some resistance but there was none. The rain of the last few weeks had softened the soil and the thistle came out in an accommodating exchange. Then, there she was, with the thing in her arms, its guilty roots covered with soil and nowhere to go.

She beat the thistle with the fork and folded it over and over, releasing its juices at each blow. She used her foot to make the bends easier and dug a hole in the garden, deep – it had to be deep to keep the restless, unfolding foetal thing down – and placed the thistle in it. She put stones on top of its body and covered it with dirt. The interment was marked by a large space, an absence in the garden: the loam newly and obviously dug over.

Jill was covered with sap and soil. She went to the porch and took her runners off, beat the loam-clogged soles on the step and went inside to shower away all traces of the sour thistle. She felt righteous and uncertain about what Annie would say. Very likely she would not notice until the morning, perhaps she would go the other way, to the garage and go out in the car early enough tomorrow not to see its absence even then. Perhaps it would be raining in the morning. Perhaps she would not notice tonight if the front porch light was turned off, or the bulb was broken or missing. A thousand times she pictured Annie walking up the steps of the porch and turning to look at where the thistle ought to have been, and running to it. Even in the dark, even unseen, she would know that it was missing and know who was guilty. She would grieve over that ugly thing.

And now it was raining so perhaps Annie would not come home at all. Perhaps she would call and say that she had met an old friend and would sleep on the friend's sofa, and when she came home in the morning, she would see the absence and would think that it was revenge. Jill would be at fault then: trivial, untrusting, unsophisticated. There would be skeins of red and purple words slung around the kitchen, they would knot up and entangle the idea of the thistle until it became everything. Jill sat in the kitchen under a single light and waited as the night drew on.

Annie was working at the local university. It was not demanding work. It was simple work that she alternately hated and tolerated. It was work that allowed her mind space to consider other things. She thought about the way the world was barely hanging together: unseen energies keeping each other in check; life, somehow, seeping through and making itself. This is what she understood. She watched the world for the chinks and mishaps, and for the subtle unfolding of the leaves and creation of one spark out of another, not 'new life' but changed energy which burst through the interstices. Disturb this meditation and she became distressed and un-herself. Most of the time, however, she managed to disguise this. Annie knew she was a weird creature, an oddball, but part of an intrinsically oddball universe. To fight it, she had found, was to make the world sour and dark.

She drove the car though the city night. It had begun to rain again and the lights became stars on the windscreen, the stop lights echoed off the road and bounced into the small puddles of water already accumulating on the footpaths. There was hardly anyone about in this part of the city. The roads were wide and the few cars quickly passed her as she drove carefully in the wet. She wondered at the other drivers' faith, or their ignorance of reduced traction on wet roads. This was a night, she thought, where everything was possible. She wanted to drive out along the highway. She knew that if she followed this city street she would, inevitably, come to the road which would take her out, past the city's horizon. She considered driving forever, not coming back, not leaving a message, not thinking ahead, not hiding her whereabouts, but not responding to beseeching calls and letters – she assumed there would be beseeching calls and letters – to come home, to come back, to make up, to live like she used to. It was a possibility.

She began to anticipate the trip. The daring of not turning off where she was supposed to turn off. The guilt of leaving that intersection, the freedom and exhilarating irresponsibility. Perhaps she would begin to drive faster along the highway, only her car lights pushing the night ahead of her. Perhaps she would end up at a seedy motel out of some old movie. She had already begun to relish the scuffed acrylic carpet creating static electricity in the room; the radio alarm set for some unlikely hour in the morning; bad paintwork; crooked bathroom tiles. There was hardly a competent tiler on the planet she thought, as she went through the intersection, not feeling guilty and not feeling irresponsible.

This day, this night, for all its irresponsibility, this non-action, this not turning right, was accomplished not with fear and guilt but with a reflection on the availability of competent tiling personnel: negligently.

Soon she was out on the highway, past the amber lights of the freeway, past the all-the-same service centres and into the countryside with its darkened petrol stations and its uncertain roads.

And then, it seemed, the other self arrived with the cool of the very early morning hours and her weariness. There were no seedy motels out here. There was nothing. Paddocks. Closed towns with closed petrol stations and coffee shops and closed accommodation with lazy 'no vacancy' signs still lit out the front. She decided, without thinking, that she would go to a friend's farm, too far out of town to have been visited before, promises notwithstanding. She didn't stop to ring Jill. She didn't stop to ring Michael and Georgia: she drove to their place as if she were in need of it.

The night was long for Jill. She stayed up watching the midnight shows on TV: *Rage* and infotainment programs about things she barely apprehended. Her limbs were getting tired and reluctant. She watched the TV because if she gave it up and went to bed she would be admitting that Annie was not coming home. By dawn there was something on the TV about water, or perhaps it was a dream. The two of them were floating down a river holding hands, lying on their backs and looking at the daylight sky. Annie was saying, very calmly, that there was a waterfall coming up soon, for sure, and then the phone rang and it seemed to Jill that the rocks were screaming. When she turned to ask Annie what it meant, she had gone and only the rush of water was left. Jill got up, uncomfortable and stiffer than usual, turned off the ranting TV, picked up her spear, and went to bed. An hour or so of sleep would be better than nothing. She had work to do in the morning. She would pretend for a while that the nothing that had happened was all right.

Annie imagined Jill, alone and fretful, her thin bones becoming stiffer and so, she rang. She let the phone ring and ring. She imagined the sound in the kitchen. She let it ring out but there was no answer. She sat in the car and waited for the sun to come up properly before she could go and greet Georgia and Michael.

She sat in the car watching the sun light up the dewy cobwebs on the fences: the red dirt going as far as she could imagine and, before long, the magpies began their gargling and quarrelling. This is enough, she thought, their black and white wings, their insolent beaks.

Annie wrote to me from Cobden saying that she'd quit her university job and had a shack in a bit of bush down the track from Michael and Georgia's. *Nothing much,* she joked. *Noxious weeds as far as the eye can see, but I'm putting in a garden. Come and stay a while,* she said. I think of my friend Jill and write to Annie that there's a lot of work on at the moment but, one day soon, I'll make it.

Phoebe's Scar

Karen Manton

Rebekah and Victoria are scampering along the edges of waves, squealing because the tide has brought in so much seaweed, they can hardly walk. They are sinking in it up to their thighs. It is winding its way along the shoreline in a thick wall held together with dumped sand. The waves push up against it and the children laugh to feel their pathway shudder.

They have been here often. They are trailing the shore that their mother used to frequent as a child. Before that their grandmother used to wander here when her husband was young, when he had just bought the block that no one else wanted, for its blackberries, impossibly steep incline and bad soil. Fifty years later, everyone wants it. And someone will be so lucky. The house will be sold on the first day of autumn. Grandma Evelyn is over it, she has enough on her plate with her own mother, Grandma Ellie, who is slowly leaving her mind and her body. And now there is no one to look after the house and the steps. Felicity and Lucas, the little girls' parents, are struggling with rent for one house, and Phoebe lives at the other end of the earth, when she is not travelling around all over the place. Phoebe has come back this summer, and that is a rare thing. There were two other sisters, but they have left the family for good, one by death, the other by choice. Grandma Evelyn cannot bear to hear their names mentioned, and though the children's tongues burn with the names and many, many questions, they obey the rule, because they fear their grandmother's sorrow, and their mother's wrath is a state to avoid.

These are the wisps of cloud in the children's minds as they stomp along through piles of beached seaweed, with their shorts pulled up to their undies. Assured in the authority of her eight years, Rebekah is telling Victoria ('who is only five') that when their mother was young, the beach had erosion markers at intervals, driven into the sand. They were so low to the ground, their mother could stand on them. With every year, the poles grew taller. It got harder and harder to stand on them. They eventually fell out of the ground because there was no more sand to keep them in. They floated out to sea on the backs of waves. Victoria is imagining hundreds of poles floating out to the horizon, when the story and her thoughts are interrupted.

Here, right under their footsteps, under the seaweed heaps, they find the strangest thing on earth. They both feel something move under their feet, something like a creature. They scream together, and stagger onto a different part of the seaweed wall. Victoria is calling out from behind her sister, not daring to look.

'What is it, what is it?'

Is it real or not? wonders Rebekah, reaching for a stick to move aside the layers of seaweed. She can see an object that seems to be dead, twisted in the middle so it is lying face down, a large sea creature of compacted seaweed, giant fish scales, seal flesh, and bleached driftwood all in one. They cannot make it out at all. Rebekah stares at it for some time. It starts to take shape.

There is a tail of scales that are slimy, pink and blue. The creature appears to be rotting. It stinks. The body is only partly covered with scales. There is a slimy flesh, like a seal's, with great chunks out of it, as if it has been hit by the propeller of a boat. A bleached arm-bone is sticking out of the sand, its hand and fingers entwined with graceful strands of seaweed that blow in the wind. The bone is covered by tiny patterns of lines and diamonds, as if it has been finely cross-hatched with a special tool. In the tail are several small fish hooks, some still with lures attached. The animal is lying face down. It has a head of seaweed hair, slimy, matted.

The children crouch down, holding their noses with one hand. The oldest one dares the younger to touch the hair, but Victoria is hesitating. So Rebekah goes ahead, scolding the younger one, 'It's dead, you fool! It can't bite!'

She stops her reproval, because she is so surprised that under her hand it feels more like human hair, like dreadlocks gone slimy. Victoria is revolted. She stands up and takes a step back, still holding her nose. It is then that the panic starts. Her toe is caught in fishing line. The older child pulls it up, and they see it leads to somewhere underneath the creature's head. Rebekah takes hold of her stick again.

'Don't, don't!' screams Victoria, who is always terribly afraid of what she cannot see.

But Rebekah will not have pity on her sister, and turns the hairy lump over.

Victoria screams, of course, and keeps on screaming until Rebekah barks at her to shut up so sharply the little girl gets a fright and gulps her exclamations and sobs back down her throat. By this time Rebekah is feeling nauseous herself. A decomposing face is looking back at her, with purple-brown lips and blackening teeth. The bottom lip is pierced with a giant hook that has also caught and entangled strands of seaweed. One glassy eye is looking out with a dead gaze from under the lashes. The other is gone beneath its closed eyelid. The creature has breasts, like a woman. There is a gold ring through one nipple. At the lower end of the belly, just above where the tail joins the torso, is a large gash, with innards partly revealed.

Rebekah staggers backwards with her stick, and throws up onto the sand. Victoria is sobbing hysterically as she runs homeward to bear the tidings to her mother who is a little white dot further up along the beach by an old sea wall.

As the sound of wails reaches her ears, Felicity Brown turns, her hand upon the large white hat with an enormous brim that is threatening to lift from her head in the breeze. Victoria looms larger, struggling with every urgent step that lowers her deep into soft, hot sand. Felicity groans to herself, and rehearses in her mind the reproach to Rebekah about being unduly harsh on her younger sibling. Her white shirt and skirt are billowing around her in the wind. She smiles at the little girl panting towards her.

Words start to fall breathlessly from Victoria's mouth, with fresh tears. She cannot get to the white, billowing shelter of her mother fast enough. And when she gets there, she cannot speak quickly or urgently enough. There is a creature. It is dead. It looks like Phoebe. Rebekah is vomiting to death.

In reality, Rebekah has no intention of dying from a bit of vomit. She is dawdling back with her stick, stopping every now and then to wash out her mouth with sea water, and spit it as far as she can towards the next significant rock or shell in her path. She has had the good sense, of course, to walk along the water's edge, where the sand is hard, and the struggle to walk is minimal. She is rehearsing in her mind what she will say to her mother about the reasons why Victoria is in tears.

When she gets to the sea wall, she throws down her stick and collapses in the sand with a loud, long sigh. Her mother is waiting for the explanation. It must be imaginative, for the disapproval to be less. Rebekah will be careful with her words. Felicity Brown is not without a keen sense of imagination. She loves a good story, and a very good story has been known to distract from possible punishments. Victoria uncurls from her mother's lap slightly, to hear the forthcoming interchange.

'There's something dead up there,' Rebekah begins, groping for the stick again and raising it to point in the direction she has come from.

'What do you think it is?' asks Felicity.

Rebekah looks to the blue sky for an answer. It seems like a perfectly hot, cloudless, sunny day. But when she arches her neck and looks back as far as she can see, there is a large, heavy cloud coming up over the hill behind them. It is about to cover the sun.

'I think it's a mermaid,' Rebekah replies.

Her mother snorts with laughter. Victoria looks at Felicity incredulously. It has been no laughing matter. Her mother is often laughing at things that are serious. It is unsettling.

'True to god,' says Rebekah, as cool and confident as a goddess herself. She calmly rises to her feet, to brush the sand from her shins. 'Funny thing is,' she goes on to say, picking up her stick and smelling the tip of it to catch a trace of any foul scent from the rotting creature she has been prodding, 'when we turned her over, she looked like Aunty Phoebe.' She looks straight into her mother's large, hazel eyes, and does not bat an eyelid.

Unbelievable, thinks Victoria.

'Well, Phoebe is not dead,' says Felicity emphatically. A great clap of thunder cracks behind them, like the whip of truth. 'And she is not anywhere near here,' she continues, rising to her feet and gathering up her towel to shake it sharply. The girls stand next to her and do the same.

'Come on, let's get moving,' the mother gives her orders, and leads the way with her determined step, the one that leaves firm and well-defined footprints in the sand for Victoria to put her own feet in. Large drops of rain are falling. Rebekah is holding her towel over her head as they walk. Felicity juts out her face to the oncoming rain and wind. The sky is darkening.

'Where is Phoebe then?' asks Victoria, leaving her footprint game to trot alongside the faster walkers.

Felicity takes a while to answer, looking for the track that will take them up the hill to the road. A branch is hanging low over the entrance. She ducks under it. The girls follow. Victoria repeats the question. Felicity stops, and catches her breath. The track is steep. She looks at her watch, and then out through the veil of twigs and leaves of trees that huddle into the cliff, to the misty grey water that was so blue before.

'Phoebe is, at this moment, under the surgeon's knife,' she says, slowly.

Victoria looks at her mother in horror. Even Rebekah does not smile and lets out a deflated little 'oh', with no hint of a suggestion that she already knows all about it. There is another burst of thunder. Felicity turns and leads them up the hill.

*

'Do you have any questions?' the surgeon asked.

Phoebe said she did not, but then again, she could not think, for fear.

He waited for her to breathe, and told her what was to happen. He would cut low, at the top of the pubic hair line, the cut would be horizontal, he would remove the growths, close her up again.

'Do you have any questions?' he asked again, kindly.

No, she did not.

The one question left she dared not ask, because she knew the answer. She had already signed off permission for her whole womb to come out if she bled too much. It was the line that had stuck in her mind for a year and kept her from this table. Instead she had gone on a merry-go-round seeking advice from many quarters, until the voices left their oracles and came to live in her head, magnifying and arguing to the point where she decided to quell their noise and give herself up to the scalpel.

The anaesthetist said, 'You will feel a tingling in your mouth, a metallic taste on your tongue,' and Phoebe did, along with a wave rolling in from the chest upwards, which somehow felt warm and icy at the same time. She thought to herself, 'I can still see the surgeon clearly,' and felt quite pleased with herself to be so wide awake, but it was precisely at that moment that everything suddenly changed. The surgeon went blurry and melted. She said 'bye', and all the masked faces were gone, closed off, just like that.

She woke up with the sound of voices, and a fierce pain in her belly. The sun had moved much lower, but she could not focus on the clock on the wall, nor the face next to the bed. Someone assured her that there was morphine at the press of her finger, but only every five minutes. A little lock stopped the constant flow. Five minutes had never seemed so long, while the lock in her gut clamped down harder and harder, like she'd been cut off there, from the navel down.

*

'Come out with me Phoebe, come right out,' the little ones were saying, insistent that their aunt risk her ankles for their joy. They were making their way out on the rock shelf, teetering on the edges of sharp limpets and coral that tormented them underfoot and brought tears to their eyes. Every time Phoebe approached them, they hurried on, yelping with the pain of their steps, and laughing.

'Come on, come on, it's not far enough yet, let's go right to the edge.'

There was no end to their energy, no end to their need to have her there with them.

'I'll watch you from the shore.' Phoebe tried to say it firmly, like a fact.

'No!' they yelled, 'you must come out with us. We'll look for crabs. We can stand at the edge of the waves.'

When does one tilt from the endless sparking of childhood into malaise, into exhaustion? Phoebe looked into Rebekah's eyes, which pleaded with her to come to the edge of the rocks. Adults are so boring, such damp blankets. The water is too cold, the weather is too wild, they have to drink their tea hot, they have to sleep in a different way, in a heavy, tired, dreamless way. They wake up weary, they do not bear the glow of expectation in their cheeks, or breathe with wonder.

'Even you Aunty Phoebe, even you are growing old,' remarked Rebekah, as she held her hand out to help steady her aunt who was thinking to herself that yes, at thirty-eight, she suddenly felt no longer young. Victoria joined them, and held Phoebe's other hand. Rebekah ran on ahead. Victoria stopped, and looked up at her aunt.

'You will always have the scar from your operation Phoebe, won't you? It's how you are now.'

'That's right.'

Phoebe crouched down with the little girl, to point out a crab, and a bright red sea anemone. Victoria was looking at her again, intently.

'We saw a dead mermaid,' she said. 'We thought she was you, but it must have been someone else.'

*

'Well for goodness' sake Felicity, did you go and see for yourself? I mean what if it was a dead body? They said it looked like a woman!' Lucas Brown was seriously freaked out.

It had all come out on the rocks, in a conversation between the girls and Phoebe, about how Rebekah had rolled the creature over, and they had seen the face of their aunt. Phoebe had thought it was funny and later re-spun the tale over cups of tea. The outcome was not what she expected. Felicity was in full flight against Lucas's suggestion that she was practically an accomplice to a local murder by not reporting a mermaid sighting from two children.

'They said it had a tail, they said it had scales, they said it was full of hooks! It was raining, Lucas, we were all about to be electrocuted in a thunderstorm! What do you want me to do, leave the children and walk halfway back up the beach to check it out? You know what they're like. If there's a shadow on the wall it's a monster and we're up half the night!'

'I'm just saying … '

'I know what you're saying and I think it's ridiculous. People do not get murdered here. Besides, I went back the next day, and there was nothing, absolutely nothing. This tea is cold.' She pushed the cup away.

Phoebe walked to the back door. She made her way down the steps her grandfather had built. Ravens were gathering in the trees around her, cawing loudly. One for suffering, two for joy, five for … she could not remember. The path to the beach was overgrown, and the gate was hanging off its hinges.

It was seven years since she had been here, and it was not until this moment, newly conscious of her belly feeling lighter within and bearing a bright pink and purple scar without, that she realised how deeply she had bonded with this beach, this outlook of her childhood. She loved its seaweed-lined shore, the moods of the sea with its patchy colours and textures, the rock shelf that meant you had to walk for miles along the beach to find a sandy gap to swim.

She hadn't noticed until now how much a part of her gaze were the Red Rocks over there on Phillip Island, and beyond, the mist-covered Nobbies, and the emerging and submerging bump of Seal Rocks that came and went like a wisdom tooth poking through the blue gums of the sea. This was the landscape she had grown up in. It was woven into conversations, events, dreams, nightmares, a thousand, thousand walks, pauses, gazes, and thoughts. The sound of it was in her sleeping, and in her breathing. It had seeped through her skin and lined the walls of her memory.

She had spent so many days travelling through other places, she had forgotten this one of her childhood footsteps in the sand, this web of interconnecting moments over years, the spinning of lives that had gone on here. She had even forgotten how it was when she left, how she had turned and gone to another corner of the earth to peel back the various skins of her memory and her heart, to the core. She felt as if she'd spent a decade shedding skins. She was very tired. She went back to the house and slept.

*

Phoebe dreamt that she was standing at the top of her grandfather's steps with Grandma Ellie, having climbed all the way up in the dark.

'I just want to see you fly,' the older woman said.

Phoebe replied, 'I cannot fly, my wings are gone.'

She shone a torch back down the way they had come. It lit up the entire pathway, and she could see that it was criss-crossed with webs too fine to pass through unscathed. Web strands were stuck to her face, to her hands, to her feet. And somewhere, in the tunnel she had escaped, her wings were still hanging, caught in that sticky web, broken off clean from her back.

*

When Phoebe woke, the sky had clouded over. She ventured back down the steps, all the same. The tide had come in, nearly all the rocks were under water. The old log that her nieces liked to climb was half submerged, along with other trees that had been moving down the line from the receding grassy slopes, collapsing with the melting, sandy cliffs into the water, skeletons of happier days, old hags with twiggy fingers and bleached bones. There were hundreds of them, dead along the beach or drowning in the water, tilting up through the sand and the waves in their various poses, like dancers who have been caught under a spell.

Phoebe sat down and waited for the storm coming in from the horizon. Rebekah and Victoria tumbled out of the track behind her and plonked themselves by her side.

She told them, 'I met a woman once, who could will the clouds towards her, fill them with her tears and watch them grow dark and heavy. She could summon the wind to carry the clouds to rain down on those who had hurt her, so that whoever had harmed her soul would feel the splat of her tears on their skin. She could tell that rain to fall harder, and harder. She could tell it to fall as hard and fast as a needle dance, and each raindrop was a prick of her pain.'

Victoria looked up at her aunt in awe. Rebekah vowed she would grow up to be such a woman. Victoria was not sure she had it in her to be such a woman, but she certainly felt she would have a lot of use for this kind of cloud magic.

The storm broke, and they hurried up the steps in lightning and rain, gasping with laughter at the sudden downpour.

*

'What are you doing?' Evelyn was standing at the open door, appalled. 'You've just had an operation. You'll get sick. Rest, they said, for six weeks. Rest! In bed!' She was peeling the shirt off Phoebe's back, pulling open drawers to find dry clothes, hurrying to the kitchen to turn on the kettle, and the central heating, and the radiator.

*

Lucas roared to see his girls so soaked. Felicity pleaded with him to lighten up. He was unbearable. Grandma Ellie was in her chair, murmuring 'Yes, yes,' as she did often, about everything from whether she liked dinner, to musings about the weather or politics. But from time to time, Evelyn felt, there was meaning to her 'yes'.

*

Phoebe was under the shower, hidden in steam. She could see her feet going up the steps, in lightning, bare, splattered with dirt and dead leaves, and rain. She remembered her grandfather as a man who set his stairs straight, just like his life. Phoebe had watched him build those steps, one by one. She had sat in the grass that was growing up through dying blackberries. She had sketched the blue wren that followed him as he worked. She had handed him the set square when he asked for it. He would say, 'Is that straight Phoebe, can you see if it is perfectly straight?' His eyesight was going, but still he worked his way down the cliff, carving out paths for his children and his children's children to walk on.

But she had no children. And the house was to be sold at the end of summer.

She was like a piece of driftwood, she felt. Her past life: childhood, adolescence, the bond between sisters that was so close-knit no one ever expected it to splinter – it all seemed so far, far away to her now, untouchable, except for a few echoes coming to her on the waves and the wind.

It was a wilder, crazier wind when they were children. It had bonded all four sisters, sweeping them along together in the one cloud of spray and sand, blowing them along the beach like those spiky grass seeds with their long legs that chase other, faster and invisible sprites. But there was a day when the wind turned, so they could not run with it, but were whittled down to nothing against it, though they had tried to stand strong, to stand together. When she looked at herself and her sisters in the quiet of her mind's eye, she saw them as clusters of tender dandelions having their fluffy heads stripped off, to end up bald stalks wobbling in the sand side by side.

Strange how memory fades, the experience passes and buries itself beneath layers and layers of other moments, like grains of sand covering a disused shell; but the scar remains. The decision is whether or not to cut it open. And even if you do, who's to say you or anyone else will be able to read your innards?

*

Rebekah was in her pyjamas, leaning against the balcony to spite her father's warning that if she did that, the whole balcony might fall down, as it was rotten. She had crept out unnoticed, to feel the wind before being shut in for the night. From her post she could see that the aunt with the scar was down at the water's edge again, arms held out to the sea.

Phoebe was unaware of the watcher up the hill. Shreds of seaweed were threaded from her fingers, flying in the wind with her hair that swirled around with her thoughts of poison and of peace.

'I am a lone woman,' she thought to herself, 'with a handful of tendrils to the past, and a head laden with snakes.'

Medusa laughed back across the waves: 'One of the snakes will be a serpent of wisdom, and with its quick strike bring the rest to their senses.'

It was then that Phoebe remembered Aurora.

*

They had met on New Year's Day, ten years ago, in the early morning before the sun crept up too high with its biting heat. Phoebe had not slept. During the night a dream had come to her that was so menacing she was still shaking when she woke. She got up and took her fear to the sea, to get the nightmare out of her head. But the awful dream would not leave, and she walked along with dread, with sinking feelings that spiralled her down. Her life was a mess. Everything was shattered. Everything was heavy – laden with the melted muck of time.

Her thoughts were interrupted by a woman who was calling out to her, hurrying back to shore from the edge of the rocks. Phoebe stopped and waited until the stranger reached her. She was an older woman. Her hair was silver and she had clear, deep blue eyes. She said she'd been out there, on the edge of the rocks, screaming at God. Her name was Aurora. She wanted to get a better look at Phoebe's hair, which was plaited and matted with salt and sand.

'I've always wanted dreadlocks,' she said.

Phoebe looked at the woman's beautiful silver hair hanging just below her buttocks and said, 'It would be a crime to do anything with that hair apart from letting it blow around wherever it wants.' But Aurora said she was determined to have dreadlocks, and she was not too old for it, being only seventy-five.

They stood side by side and spoke for an hour, about the twists and turns of life, of living and loving and leaving. Phoebe had never seen eyes so blue, or hair so silver, or heard such a divine laugh. She wondered if she were standing by an angel, and if so, where were her wings.

The woman told stories: of her beautiful grandson who had a rare condition that hindered his sight but not his spirit; of her backpacker travels around the world in the last five years; of adventures in yachting, which she had taken up at seventy, when she decided to become a deckhand. Aurora was a free spirit not to be bridled. She wanted to know what were Phoebe's dreams, because she believed they would all come true, fortune or not.

'You will have a wonderful life, and you will do all that you want to do,' she said to Phoebe, looking into her eyes with her own clear blue ones, like it was a promise, or a knowing, and then she was gone.

Phoebe had never felt so affected by a total stranger. She walked on along the beach transformed, and never forgot the woman. She took the memory of that one hour with her wherever she went, as a kind of blessing that never lost its windswept touch.

*

Two dolphins are rolling in towards the rocks. Phoebe has not seen a dolphin at this beach since her tenth birthday. The rising sun is bright on the water, and warm on her feet. Her scar is itching. Suddenly one of the dolphins shoots up into the air, vertical. Again and again it comes rocketing out of the water. Victoria calls to her aunt. She is labouring across last night's heaved up sea garden, to the rocks. Her pyjamas are covered in little seaweed leaves when she gets there. She is captivated by the performance, which ends almost as soon as she arrives.

'Let's walk to where the mermaid was,' she says, taking Phoebe's hand and leading her away.

Rebekah has already been back and left her stick upright, with a flag of seaweed hanging from it, to mark where she claimed was the exact spot of their strange discovery. There is no sign of the creature.

'What do you think happened to her?' Phoebe asks.

'I think she has put herself back together,' says Victoria, 'I think she has taken herself back to where she came from.'

The little girl goes off skipping, and Phoebe thinks of spiky grass seeds hurrying across the sand.

If You Don't Like it Leave

Alejandra Martinez

It's hot and my car is old and doesn't have airconditioning. I'm stuck in traffic. If I hadn't agreed to see my dad today I wouldn't be here; instead I'd be lying in front of the fan reading a novel. It has taken me thirty minutes to get from Annandale to the footbridge at Sydney Uni. My dog Carla sits next to me panting, her head stuck out the window, waiting for a whiff of air to come her way. She is a good dog, patient. She doesn't bark, even out of annoyance. I feel my blood boiling. I'm annoyed at being stuck in the traffic. I'm annoyed at my dad for having no friends, for having no life after my mum died. For depending on my sister and me to give him a reason to live. If he had his own life, I wouldn't be stuck in this traffic jam now, sweating, feeling my bum stuck on the vinyl seat. Not even the radio works in this old car.

The car in front puts his indicator on and changes lanes. Why bother? That lane isn't going any faster. My view has changed. YSM 251 has left and I have a Subaru stationwagon in front of me. Staring me in the face are the words, IF YOU DON'T LIKE IT LEAVE, with a picture of the Australian flag.

I feel a shudder go through my whole body. If you don't like what? The beaches, the government, being stuck in traffic on Parramatta Road on a Saturday afternoon?

I feel scared of people who think this way.

Whatever happened to, 'If you don't like it, change it'? Maybe I could get a sticker for my car with that. I feel personally affronted by this sticker. Why does it hurt me so much?

I look at the Footbridge Theatre to see what's on. I've crossed that footbridge so many times. My student days flash before me. Last minute essays, no money to buy the textbooks. I'm still poor. I don't like being poor, does that mean I should leave too? Where would I go if I did leave? I definitely couldn't go back to South America. My Spanish is not good enough to get a job and my English is missing the grammar needed to teach it. Anyway I don't want to leave. I'm happy here. I have my dog, my old car, and my part-time job at the neighbourhood centre. I'm fulfilled. My glass is half full as the saying goes. I don't have a boyfriend, I don't have children and I still haven't written that novel that sits in my head, but that is no reason to leave.

The traffic begins to move. I wish I had brought some water. Carla is starting to get restless. 'We're nearly there,' I say, patting her.

Finally I turn into Glebe Point Road. The familiar cafés greet me. Many of them I know intimately. I've written essays at those tables. And dreams, dreams that spoke to me during my time in Jungian analysis.

The traffic is still a bit slow. The markets are on in the school, that's why it's so slow. Gleebooks comes into view. Hours of my life have been spent there. Sometimes, the shop was almost a refuge.

Should I stop to buy some pastries? Will my dad have anything to eat?

He'll probably say, 'I don't have anything because I haven't been shopping yet. I couldn't leave the house because I didn't know when you were coming.'

I love the inner city. I grew up in Australian working-class suburbia; fibro houses in a cul-de sac, the sound of lawnmowers seeping through Sunday morning dreams, kids hanging out at the local fish and chip shop. Footwear was thongs;

dining out, the local Chinese. Women talked Avon and men footy. As a teenager I hated it. I found it alienating, a sense of displacement raged inside me. But I couldn't leave. It must have been worse for my parents. They didn't even speak English.

We had just left one country because of political turmoil; we weren't about to leave again.

Sometimes we don't have choices. I wanted to get out of the car and tell that to whoever was driving that Subaru.

What would make someone really feel that you had to love Australia? Why did they love it? Does my dad love it? He doesn't want to go back to South America. And yet he has no life here. He sits in his Department of Housing unit, he eats, watches TV, reads, sleeps. He goes to the shop to buy more food to eat. He waits for my sister and me to visit him. We drink coffee with him, we eat, we talk, we go. He closes his door. What would he do if he went back? Would his life come back to him? His old life wouldn't be waiting for him after thirty years; it would no longer fit him.

I see a parking spot and accelerate to get to it. Lucky to get a parking spot on Glebe Point Road on a Saturday afternoon. One reason not to leave.

I open the passenger door for Carla. She jumps out with relief. 'Now some water for you.'

I go into the nearest café and sit outside, Carla by my side. I've been here before and they always bring me water for Carla.

The waitress comes to take my order. She has an English accent. A traveller on a working holiday. I wonder if she likes it here or if she should leave.

'I'll have a latte and a glass of water. Can I also get some water for my dog please?'

'Sure,' the English girl smiles at me.

Carla and I quench our thirsts. She can now relax under the table. It's cool.

I sip my coffee and watch the passers by. I love doing this. I could spend all day sitting in cafés watching people. It's reassuring that the world exists, that there are other people looking for ways to spend their Saturday afternoons. There are lots of children today. Some of them want to pat my dog and talk to me. I love the way young children have no sense of private space. Some parents are embarrassed and apologise for this.

I see someone I went to uni with. She waves at me and comes over to say hello.

'How are you?' she asks.

'Good and you?'

'Really well.'

'What have you been up to?' I ask her.

'I'm preparing for an exhibition next month so I'm madly trying to finish a couple of paintings.'

'Oh, that sounds great, good luck with it.'

'Thanks,' she says. 'It was nice to see you.'

'Yeah, and you,' I lie.

'Ok, bye.'

'Bye.'

I watch her walk away. She is one of the few who can continue playing into adulthood. Her parents' wealth will always be there to catch her. She has no reason to leave.

I finish my coffee and go in and pay.

I make my way to the cake shop. I get four croissants and two Portuguese custard tarts. I don't like the traditional Australian custard tarts. Thank goodness there are shops that cater for my woggy palette and thank goodness all these people haven't left with their great food.

I drive my old car to my dad's. He moved here after my mum died to be close to his daughters. After years of waiting he was given this unit.

I park the car and Carla and I make our way to the door. The blinds are closed. My dad likes to keep the world out. I knock on the door. I hear his steps as he gets up to open the door.

'Hello.' We kiss each other on the cheek. Carla is excited to see him. He pats her and talks to her as if she were a child.

'I have the coffee on the stove, I was just waiting for you to get here to turn it on.' I look at the old percolator sitting on the stove. I've had so many coffees from that percolator.

'I've just had a coffee,' I say, 'but I guess I could have another.' I'm a coffee addict. Coffee warms me emotionally, like getting into bed with clean sheets. Those pathetic little creature comforts that give one a sense of primal security.

'I bought some croissants Papa.'

'That's good because I couldn't go to the shops, I didn't know what time you would be here and I didn't want you to get here and me not to be here.'

'How have you been Papa?'

'Good and you?'

'Good, what have you been doing?'

'Lots of cleaning today, it just gets so dusty here.'

'Have you been using the computer?'

'A little, it gets a bit hard with the arthritis, but I have been reading the Uruguayan and Argentinian papers. It's very good this Internet. All these people who have lost their money, it's very sad. Many lost their life savings, banging the doors of the banks they were.'

'They're all the middle classes, they'll survive,' I say.

He serves the coffee and we make our way to the table by the window. I put the croissants and the Portuguese tarts on a plate. Carla sits by my side dribbling in anticipation of what little morsel may come her way. There is a beautiful frangipani tree outside the window but the blind is down.

I open the blind.

My dad looks at me. 'You know the neighbours can see in.'

'I don't care, we have nothing to hide.'

'Yes but they will see us. The girl next door has a boyfriend on drugs. He will know I have a computer and a television to steal. You know yesterday they had a fight. I could hear the shouting until three in the morning. The children were crying. Terrible. *Pobrecitos inocentes.*'

This is not the first time. 'They'll probably take them from her eventually,' I say.

He shakes his head. Is he thinking about his own life? He lost his parents at the age of six.

The children next door can't like their life. Can they leave? Someone will make that decision for them.

'Nice croissants. Where did you get them?'

'The cake shop next to the Lebanese.'

'Your mum liked that shop too. Her favourite were the almond croissants.' He is more nostalgic than usual today.

'Laura rang me yesterday,' he says, changing the topic. 'She says she wants to go to Italy. To study. Why does she have to go so far to study? What is wrong with Australian universities?'

'There's nothing wrong with Australian universities, she's just bored with her life here.'

'How can she be bored? She has a good life. A good job, a nice car.'

'I know Dad, but she's looking for some inner meaning, I guess.' My sister is always looking for the next adventure.

We sit in silence for the next few minutes. Boredom and the seeking of fulfilment are luxuries that my Dad never had. His life was about survival.

'What are you having for dinner tonight?'

'I don't know Papa, I haven't thought about it.'

'I'm going to make *milanesas'* snitzels, he says, proudly. I bought them at the butcher's already crumbed. All I have to do is fry them. I know they won't be as good as what Mama made but they will be good. Then I will make mashed potatoes and a salad and drink a nice glass of wine. Do you want to stay for dinner?'

'No, I can't, I'm going to see a movie with a friend.'

'What movie?'

'It's a documentary about eating fast foods and how bad it is for you.'

'What do you want to see that for? Of course it's bad to eat that rubbish.'

'I know, but it's more than that, it's a critique of multinationals.'

'That's good.' He gives it his socialist approval.

I remember the political films of the seventies. In community centres in lost Australian suburbs, South American refugees held functions showing films about the dictatorships from which they had just escaped. The functions were family affairs. The children would run around playing, suddenly stopping to watch someone crying desperately on the screen. When we got bored we continued playing.

We ate *empanadas* and drank lemonade. The adults talked a lot after the films. Sometimes someone would bring a guitar and they would sing songs we couldn't understand. Some of the adults cried.

'Do you want another coffee?' my dad asks.

'No, thanks. I've already had too many today.'

'This is my first coffee today, I didn't want to have one until you got here.'

My visit is the highlight of his day. He even plans his coffee-drinking around it.

My mother used to organise their social life. When she died his social life died too.

'What about a cup of tea?'

'No thanks Papa. I'll have to get going, I want to take Carla for a walk before I go to the movies.'

'How's your car going?'

'It's going, struggling but going.'

'You'll have to get a new car soon.'

'I know Papa, I know.'

I get up to go. My dad gets up. He walks me to the door. We kiss goodbye.

'*Adios mija.*' *Mija* is a term of endearment that Uruguayan parents use for their children. It immediately caresses me with memories of my childhood.

'*Chau Papa.*' He bends down to pat Carla.

I step outside and he closes the door. I walk over to the car and Carla and I get in and drive away. As I go past, I see his window next to the frangipani tree. The blind is closed and I can't see in.

Here is the Heartflower

Gillian Mears

How alive the leaven-starter for sourdough bread remains is very dependent on who is attending to its needs. If the person's assiduous, the starter can last many years, and if the instructions for its wellbeing have been faithfully transmitted, even generations. On the other hand, if the person is too fastidious, something of that quality can ruin the ferment and the bread made will be boring.

This is the problem, thinks the yoga teacher taking down his jar of starter from a kitchen shelf, with his marriage to Jeannie. In less than three years it has become too still, too structured, with an ominously quiet centre. Although he has to give his yoga class in less than an hour, he carries the jar over to the sink, unsure what he'll find after so many days of neglect.

Richard Elver isn't a man who must constantly check his appearance in mirrors or glass surfaces or windows, something in him accepting that beauty was a gift given long ago.

'You make me feel like a paedophile,' a lover used to say of him at fifty, because even as Richard's hair grows greyer, his large head on such a slender neck contributes to a never-ending air that he is somehow still a child.

Is it any wonder that students who regularly attend Richard's Thursday afternoon class fall at least a little bit in love?

Sometimes, a student, as in the case of Jeannie, will fall under his spell the moment she sights him poised in half lotus in front of the candle before the class begins. Others remain steadfast until his hand touches their sternum to emphasise its importance in warrior pose.

The men who attend regularly are possibly themselves like Richard – as in, now with women but ever aware that once they were young and willingly attractive to men, moving their feet faster along the footpath as the music from The Midnight Shift on Oxford St beckoned them for a dance.

The late August weather, so preternaturally warm, means that the starter already needs much more attention.

'Come here then, Lawrence of Arabia,' Richard says, due to the cloth lid over the jar having the appearance of a Bedouin. 'Ugghh!' For in the neglect of the starter that always occurs now he lives partly in Jeannie's inner-city flat, part-time in his own place in a patch of bush about two hours north if the traffic's reasonable, mould has overtaken the jar. He examines it with interest and smiles. Every now and then, according to the bread-making lore of his first boyfriend Patrick Lindeman, it doesn't hurt for the starter to go this black and mysterious with neglect. Once resuscitated, the very best bread is always guaranteed.

This starter is a blend that began in America, or so Patrick's story went, his maternal forbears keeping it alive no matter what the hazards encountered. To stop it from freezing, Patrick's great grandmother used to rest it between her bosoms, over her heart, which is why, Patrick used to say with his widest grin, it made bread of such a unique tang. 'She'd have a heart attack if she knew what ingredient we've added.'

Richard stirs the starter. Uh-oh, compost needs emptying, but no time now so tipping out the excess, he shuts his ears to Jeannie's imagined voice of complaint accusing him of turning her flat into a brothel.

Using one of his old Aunt Reenie's teaspoons – how did it get to be sitting in Jeannie's cutlery drawer? – he scoops in the fresh flour, two, no, make it three teaspoons. Next he takes a fresh chopstick with which to vigorously stir. 'Cha! Cha!' adding his voice; moving his body in a drag-heel dance step. 'Cha! Drag-heel, Cha!' Once again he stirs briskly before transferring it to a jar sparkling from the dishwasher he'd vowed at first never to use.

Neglected sourdough starter always makes Richard remember the last time he sucked Patrick off. Patrick, already breaking the law with a fourteen-year-old called Elainie, hadn't really wanted him but had allowed it as part of a farewell fuck.

Patrick and Elainie had stayed together long enough to have two babies. When Richard was getting away from heroin, they'd turned out to be his best friends. He can remember sleeping on their lounge-room floor and two little girls swarming over him as if he was land. That would've been around the time of early NA meetings after the overdose.

When Richard first made the switch to women he recalls that shocking delight followed shocking delight. Kissing his first girlfriend was like biting into white bread smothered in cream and honey; flimsy, yet at the same time capable of shredding the skin off the top of your mouth or dick. In Paris there was the woman he was using with from the Bastille. His skin had handled the gauge of the bull-size needles less well than hers. What he learnt with her is that kindness can occur in unexpected ways. She'd found veins for him that would still work, slipping in the needle with the tenderness of a mother. For his birthday in bed she'd made miso soup and tiny nori rolls in tempura, before crouching over his face to offer herself as dessert.

Richard's thoughts return to Jeannie. Since turning her fully, even fanatically macrobiotic, she'd surely taste neutral yet nourishing too in the way of a well-prepared autumn vegetable casserole? One day soon, he resolves, he'll rake up the courage to put his theory to the test with his tongue.

These last thoughts have a fragile quality, however, for Richard isn't very sure that he wants to be a married man anymore; let alone a man who has relinquished the occasional beat along the river. 'You'll live,' he says to the starter.

Everything else is already packed in the car ready for his days with Jeannie in his house.

He leaps down the stairs, more ballet dancer now, not spilling a drop of starter or slopping it up the sides. With a final athletic curve he slips into the car and placing the jar where most people would carry a can of Coke or cold drink is away at last.

Oh, plenty of time to unlock and set up before any students arrive. Plenty of time to ease the coiling energy those two reckless coffees of early in the day have set in motion underneath his ribcage.

*

He crashes his car, looking at that woman on the footpath as he reverse parks. Surely it's Elainie he has seen? So that the young girls, with the long legs, must be Ajita and Ruby Ann? For a moment they move out of sight and he feels a sadness that is like a prefiguration of a greater sadness yet to come.

'Richard!' Elainie's at his window. 'How's that for timing. Thought you would've at least learnt to drive by now,' leaning in to kiss. Because the kiss is slightly crooked, landing in a place so strangely high near his eye, for the rest of the day he will feel that his face resembles a portrait by Picasso.

'It is you! Elainie! So this must be Ruby Ann then, and Ajita? How amazing.'

The girls peer in. He hasn't seen them since Ajita was say four, Ruby Ann two but immediately he sees that just doesn't matter. An instant friendliness springs back and forth between them all.

'Couldn't find a number for you Richard in the phone book,' Elainie's saying, 'so on the weekend we walked up here. Ruby Ann saw the flyer for your class on the noticeboard.'

'Even said you were the guy in the loincloth doing the pose.' Ajita loads her voice with sisterly scorn.

'Well,' Richard lowers his voice to a suitably modest level. 'She's right, that is me.'

'See! Told you I remembered Richard.'

'That's an earthly impossibility Ruby Ann.'

'Girls, girls.'

'Are you staying close by?' Richard leaves the car.

'Just round two corners.'

'Wish I'd known. You could've stayed at Jeannie's with me. I'm married now.'

'Yeah, you sent us an invitation.'

'And none of you came.'

'Look anyway, we're on holidays … '

'From Melbourne?'

'Yeah and really would love to catch up.'

'Well why not come for the weekend to my place in the bush? Oh, wait on though,' he adds remembering the recent edict from Jeannie about checking first before visitors come. 'I'll just ring Jeannie, except oh, can't, battery's flat.'

'Here, use ours,' the girls wave cell phones that look like confectionary from outer space.

Elainie grimaces. 'You know Patrick barely sees them, not even for their birthdays, but he buys them things like that. Still basically bi y'know. So I hear.'

'Ah, no, no answer. Look it doesn't matter, come anyway. You've got a car have you?'

'Everything,' say the girls. 'Camping gear! Food!'

'Well want to come to this class I'm just about to teach?'

'We've got to eat, and drink,' Elainie pulls her hair back and holds it in a ponytail. 'Unbelievable how warm it is for August.'

'There's that great old Macro café still. Only a bit corrupted. Serving palm sugar in puddings.'

'Richard! You're not still Mr MacroDoc are you?'

'Oh,' he gives his most whimsical smile. 'Wif old friends? Always. Someone's got to show the way. Keep the true fire burning.'

*

By the following morning the sourdough starter's alive and well again. 'See this?' he says to Ajita. 'Watch, OK?' He taps the side of the jar. 'Like galaxies exploding, the ferment!' He shakes it to exaggerate the effect even further. 'Stars being born. But Patrick must still make his own bread?'

'You have to be kidding. Dad's a degenerate.'

'Really? You mean he really hasn't kept the starter that had been in his family for nearly two hundred years?' But the girl just looks at him.

'Well believe me or not, your father made a great bread, with a particular tang but not at the expense of, oh, a deliciously wheaty flavour.'

'Not boring poor Ajita with macrobiotics at this hour are you,' says Jeannie, drifting in from her bedroom. Apart from her curatorial work at a photography gallery, she's also begun to teach a few beginner yoga classes. Her leanness is such an echo of Richard's that they're often mistaken for brother and sister. Oh-oh, she thinks. Richard's wearing his blue cotton bread-making apron in which he looks ready for *Play School.* 'Seems pretty good though,' she says peering into the jar of starter as if she can use its fermentation to scry the future. 'Maybe we could use up the left-over loaf I made? Anyone else for sourdough toast?'

'Yes please!' exclaims the other girl, coming in with her mother through the back garden door from where the tent was pitched last night. 'To warm us up! We froze in there this morning, didn't we Lainey?' Leaning in to her mother's hip.

'Really,' says Richard, 'Cold? Well sleep inside,' he suggests.

'Not for me,' says Elainie. I love camping.'

'Well for the girls. They could have the bed in the spare room. That'd be OK wouldn't it Jeannie?'

Although this is Jeannie's room, where she always sleeps alone, she nods her acquiescence, even going so far as to gild her voice with false pleasure. 'No worries. There's a doona in there that could melt the polar icecap overnight.'

As soon as she can she detaches herself from the breakfast activities. Going into her room to prepare it for the girls she pauses momentarily, making the mistake of looking at herself in the mirror. At this time of day her throat is now so weathered it looks as though it's been in a fire. Could it be cancer? I mean, her thoughts run, what'd be so odd about that? With so many of the luminary figures of the old macro world dead or dying of different variations of the disease they once claimed with such airy certainity that they could cure, holding up their cigarettes so as to only inhale the purple yin smoke?

On the other hand, Jeannie roughly yanks her sheets off the bed, how can it be that almost all of Richard's old compatriots from NA days are so fantastically well-preserved and good-looking? Got to be more to it than miso soup hasn't there? Jeannie pulls a face at herself. 'You old sourdough,' she says to her reflection before seeking out a beautiful sundried, sun-faded pair of crimson sheets. She plumps up pillows. From a chest that smells of camphorlaurel, she brings out her favourite blankets, putting the one with the red stitchery heart on top. She leaves the doona folded at the bottom. Now the girls will be warm won't they?

She can hear Richard giving instructions to them as he begins to make bread. 'This is the key to success,' he's saying. 'And I don't just mean that I'm using freshly ground flour from biodynamic wheat. No, it's what you put into your kneading. This is why some loaves are exceptional. This is where the true goodness of the bread is formed. This is the heart flour.' Jeannie recognises the words. Hadn't she become even more enraptured with her yoga teacher at his quarterly change-of-season bread-making workshop? But that was before they lived together and that was before Richard asked one morning had she too noticed how each grain of wheat is like a little girl made miniature. When Jeannie had looked puzzled Richard had said, 'You know what I mean don't you? A girl,' shyly placing his hand over the crotch of his jeans.

Jeannie comes back out. Ajita's having a turn at kneading. A suitably exotic name, Jeannie thinks, but for godsake, am I the only person in the house who realises what the name actually means? She stands scrutinising the strange tableau, the girls and the man in front of the strange kitchen cupboards.

Huge timber uprights painted uneven shades of blue reach into the cathedral ceiling. The cupboard below, also painted blue, has had at some stage an amateur mosaicist at work on the top. Old food and flour get caught in between the pieces of smashed saucers and glass in a way that keeps Jeannie always on semi-alert for the first signs of a salmonella outbreak. Only the smell inside the cupboard is consoling with its fragrance of old wood. China stacked inside from deceased aunties holds memories, Jeannie's sure, of many good meals, wispy laughter, secret jokes against the men, while the Sunday roast bubbled and sang and someone stirred a dark gravy into the sweet miracle it always was. Her aunt's old dinner set takes up the left side of the cupboard, Richard's Aunt Reenie's the right. Clichés of an auntly kind run through her mind. Time to call it a day. A clean break might be best. Lovie?

If she does give up trying to be married to such a difficult, past middle-age man, she'll miss neither the cupboard nor his house, with all its solar rules and regulations. How could she ever have believed, back when Richard Elver was her elegant yoga teacher, that he could be a safe and wise harbour for the rest of her life? Would he stop talking if she goes outside to make great melancholic hooms sitting inside the empty corrugated iron water tank?

So much for this being the weekend set aside for them to speak clearly about this feeling growing in them both that marriage after all was a really bad idea. I mean what were they thinking signing the marriage certificate: that a recently lesbian-identified woman and her once gay ex-junkie yoga teacher were really going to live happily ever after? She's embarrassed now by memories of the wedding down at Blackwattle Bay on dusk.

The sudden thought of her last girlfriend before the switch to Richard makes Jeannie lean as if in pain against the wall. Maybe time passing has exaggerated the loveliness? But anyway, always now that woman's quality as of a warm breeze as they sipped tea and looked out through a window to the harbour.

'I still eat sugar every now and then,' Elainie's confessing. 'But we might go for a swim I think.'

'A swim!' Jeannie comes across to boil a bancha. 'You know there was ice down on the river's edge three weeks ago.'

'The girls don't mind. In fact seeing them under a waterfall on our way over I couldn't believe it. Their lips went blue. Had to give them chocolate that day Ricardo. But not normally. And they're funny like that – not really that interested in sweet things.'

'We're Savoury Girls,' announces Ajita, reappearing with towels.

'Well I'll come down. Show you the best rocks for a sunbake,' Richard unties his apron.

'I might start thinking about lunch? I think?' says Jeannie but it's as if no one has even heard her, she is so obviously irrelevant to the inchoate surge of emotions connecting the children and Elainie to Richard; their history feeling as old as the history of leavened bread itself.

*

Although she'd resolved not to, the moment the rice is simmering, Jeannie returns in her mind to certain scenes from last night. The girls are very beautiful and like their mother, will turn into beautiful women. Anyone would say so. They have such a glossiness and every limb is in fantastic long proportion to the next. Because Richard had both wood stove and open fire roaring last night there hadn't been a need for many clothes.

Well this is how it was, remembers Jeannie. First of all Ruby Ann was doing yoga in shorts, all legs, all legs, all immaculate skin and hair, standing on her head. A rivalry was springing up between her and Ajita to gain Richard's attention. Didn't they know their father used to be Richard's boyfriend? Or was that part of the closeness?

Ajita, wearing the most miniature of pink skirts butted in to say she'd show Richard her best asana. Cross legged in front of him she'd moved her heels together, knees almost touching the ground. However the child's skirt was so short she couldn't maintain this without her pants showing. Still, directly facing Richard, she kept on trying to do the position at the same time as keep her skirt down.

Richard had given one of those smiles Jeannie has come to dread. 'Careful,' he'd said to Ajita, smiling right at the girl.

Jeannie cuts vegetables the way she learned in one of Richard's cooking workshops. Half-moons of parsnip slide from the knife blade. I mean, am I the only one wondering if the beauty of Patrick's children reminds Richard of other times? She matchsticks some carrots, the knife savage on Aunt Hope's old round chopping board. Where's the tahini bottle been put? What've they done with the ginger?

The oil's almost hot enough to begin frying when they all come bursting back into the house through the kitchen's French doors.

Because the sun's drenching across the floorboards as if it's a forest not a kitchen and maybe because Jeannie looks so thin and sad, the girls begin the dance that may be going to end this fledgling marriage between a once-gay man and his nearly forty-year-old wife. The girls' sarongs, only loosely knotted, come spontaneously and simultaneously off, so that coloured cloth becomes part of their whirl. Their skin's as smooth and brown as eggs from a country town where the hens are still allowed to roam and scratch in old flowerbeds gone to seed.

The dance of Ajita and Ruby Ann is as beautiful as any ever seen. Like colts, like fillies after a storm, they prance and lift their knees up high. They toss their river-tangled hair and faster they go. To the watchers the dance holds history. It is fourteen-year-old Salome's dance before she knew she'd be carrying in John the Baptist's head on a platter. It is the pair of sisters carved onto the sides of tombs, preparing the prince for his virgin bride, their stone thighs full of knowledge.

You just want to watch, Jeannie thinks. Looking has made her feel dreamy and vast as she tries to remember the girl of long ago she once was with bud-flower breasts on the brink of bloom, and the hairlessness that allows no clothes. But please. She looks away. Why, please, doesn't their mother tell them to put on their clothes? Yet to commence cooking seems an insult so she switches off the gas. It's at this moment that Jeannie detects the mottled pattern of light sunburn over the girls; all over them. She looks up through the high window with coloured glass in the shape of toy sailing boats.

Oh, she wants to moan with pain, thinking of Richard lying down on the sunbaking rock, naked as well. She looks down at the jar of starter full of its ancient, American frontier, Patrick Lindeman bacteria. At the sight of Richard's face, for finally Jeannie has dared a glance, she puts her hand around the jar and walking to the sink and removing the rubberband head-dress, patiently flushes it away. Patience is required because the water pressure is so low.

You want to touch. Richard is so dazed that he sits down in the red, wind-trembled chair closest to hand. You want to touch. When his camping holiday with their father had reached the desert, they'd discovered how to get cold water without a fridge; it was a kind of miracle, water without a lid left in the truck's shade becoming icy. Patrick's daughters are like that water. Yes it is so, Richard thinks, just effortlessly, naturally refreshing.

The dance of God in girls, that's what he feels he's in the presence of, and his spine cracks as he stretches up as if to touch the dance itself. But more than that, he realises he wants to just run a finger, a hand, along that perfect curve, and that one, going past. As you would a statue. He wills himself not to look between their legs but sees anyway.

The girls go in a circle, faster now, faster. He wants to rattle kitchen spoons, hit his bread tins like drums. Rah! He wants to yell, pulling off his own sarong. Like King David dancing until his wife looked away in shame, he would leap and his hips would move. Rah! Or he would be for Jonathan, on all fours with his head down. Richard seeks a more stable position in the chair, crossing his legs until each foot droops over each opposite thigh like creatures of their own independent thought. He would be a girl, only his eyes visible above the veil.

'Hey! You two!' Elainie claps her hands together. 'That's enough now!' She's smiling, as if this event is a perfectly normal one in the day of being the mother of these two.

The girls circle once, twice more, giggling, lighter, flitting like little birds now as their sarongs are again knotted. Ajita, calculates Richard, is just about two years younger than Elainie was when she first began to climb out her bedroom window to meet up with Patrick. Two or three years later wasn't it that Elainie was pregnant with Ajita?

*

Crackle crackle, crackle Jeannie's tri-coloured nituke vegetable chips are a great success, everyone eating with gusto, the mouths of the girls shining with the mustard-seed oil Jeannie used for the frying. Without seeing if anyone else would like seconds, Richard takes the final serve of brown rice for himself. Once a smacko, always a smacko, thinks Jeannie.

'A full moon tonight, isn't it Jeannie?' Richard tips the rest of the chips into his bowl.

'Well, an old full moon.'

'Do you two know what keeps the earth stable?'

'Gravity?!' They say as one.

'Uh-uh. It's the moon. The moon, that's what keeps the earth from wobbling,' and picking up a juggling ball in his fingers he attempts to demonstrate what he means. 'See, like this? Because the moon's passing around earth every twenty-eight days.'

This day of the dance also begins to pass. It smells summery, of honey, everyone slapping dead the early horseflies out on the western verandah. On dusk, the girls brush their hair and Ruby Ann catches a firefly in a jar before letting it go. The idea of an outside fire doesn't eventuate as everyone except Jeannie agrees that an early night is a good idea.

*

It has been such a long time since Jeannie shared a bed with this thin man her husband that upon entering Richard's room she feels panic rising up her throat. He's already in bed, reading by candlelight to save the solar battery. Taking off her clothes, she comes into the bed as he puts down his book.

Something she's never told Richard is how she became the scandal of her small country town, falling pregnant to old Bert Winkley. She'd had the abortion late one Monday afternoon, her tight-lipped parents driving her to the Gold Coast after she'd won Champion Girl Rider under-fifteen, riding one of Bert's horses. There were mumblings that the old bugger should be prosecuted, but nothing ever came of it. When 'the old bugger' died some twenty or more years later, Jeannie travelled all the way back to the tiny town to go to his funeral. Another old horseman in a hat, a Winkley cousin, had sung 'Danny Boy' in a voice so limpid it was impossible to contain her sobbing as instead of frankincense, she smelt horse sweat and whisky, calculating that her child with Bert would've been twenty years old.

Although they've never taken any contraceptive measures, Jeannie has never fallen pregnant to Richard.

She feels how stiff contained grief grows and is glad when Richard half drapes his body over hers.

'You're sad,' he says. 'I can sense it here,' he brushes a hand over the collarbone she broke falling off one of Bert's ponies.

She says nothing. This is very like nature, though, she feels, these two ageing bodies, this way they lie so patiently together; a twig against leafy ground; a creek running through native grass; their breath falling into synchronicity. Just a little now, their bodies are beginning to move, and though neither fully understands the nature of the other, the sadness moving in her meets the different sadness moving in him.

As unceremonious as ever as a lover, when Richard blows out the candle, snuffing out the wick with spit, Jeannie's sadness trembles on rage. Which one's beneath you, she wants to scream. Little Ruby Ann or Ajita whose name means the feminine ejaculate of young women? As he scrambles aboard like a thin boy trying to tame a wild pony.

In order to contain a bitterness so violent it's a wonder it's not spraying out to stain Richard's bedsheets, she turns herself not into one of the girls but into herself at that age. It's the history in old Bert Winkley's hands, it's the history in an old horseman's heart she's moving beneath.

However, nothing Jeannie's thinking is anything close to why Richard has begun his own urgent memories. In his mind he too is young again, less than twenty. Patrick has been swimming and his left buttock muscle gleams with seawater. Next he's pushing Richard down on coastal rock to expose the left side of his neck. Now he's letting Patrick's sharp teeth bite him in such a way over his jugular that surely the rockpool close by turns red with blood not sunset. Whoosh, whoosh, the waves breaking; whoosh, the sighing waves disguising his sighs of shivery pain; his neck the offering; his body the tight and winking mystery waiting. Patrick, saying ah, you greedy ..., putting his whole hand into Richard's mouth, forcing his lips to become dark and pink and more female than was possible in real life.

Finally, the bellies of Richard and Jeannie, so alive and uncoiled with old distress and desire, begin to act in the way that's impossible when you're a child; their thoughts carried away in the sounds they cannot muffle though the girls might lie whispering head to toe on the crimson sheets of Jeannie's bed down below.

*

'Are you going to get the stove going or will I?' Richard can't remember either of them lighting the half-melted candle.

'It's only seven o'clock!' After last night's explanations, she thinks she still loves him but isn't sure. The long flame of the candle trembles. Jeannie lights a new candle before blowing out the old. Picking up a knife covered in candle wax she trims away some soft wax.

'But I wanted the house to smell of fresh sourdough. For their last day. A little honey-coloured cob loaf.'

'I thought they were staying until Tuesday?'

'Didn't I say? Elainie thinks they should head off. City people are like that. The bush delights them briefly and then they're bored. That old Chinese proverb?'

'The wind got up in the night and took our plans away.'

'Yes, and it's a good thing. Unpredictability. Constantin Brancusi, I used this at the end of yoga the other night. Well he had this theory about life. How it has to be in constant ferment. Can't be safe. Always changing. His sculptures depended on that alone, he said. We have to be a bit more like sourdough starter. It's hard to explain but you get what I mean don't you?'

'There is no starter,' without planning Jeannie speaks. She takes some of the soft trimmed beeswax in her fingers and begins to knead.

'Sorry?'

'Yesterday, you know? I tipped it down the sink.'

Richard lies back down on his pillow.

A sad-happy feeling she secretly calls sapliness – the sap of a life running sweetly, running sadly, is growing. 'Because really, I don't think we can stay together? Do you?' She folds the piece of wax into a heart. From the heart she pulls out a stem. Even though it will accentuate the way her skin is leaving the bones of her face she slides up off the safety of her pillow to sit on top of Richard.

'That sourdough starter was an heirloom Jeannie,' says Richard. 'It began as Patrick's ancestors began their crossing of the great prairies in a covered wagon.'

'Maybe if their seeds were available from Greenpatch.'

'What?'

'Heartflowers. Well anyway, I've made us one.'

He tilts his head sideways on its thin neck. Because this makes him look like a sad, pretty boy from another land, she shimmies her shoulderblades. Her breasts, which are just large enough, move. There's the scar from her long defunct nipple piercing, he sees. Her left ear also, punctured by about six obsolete holes and for a moment, as her eyes meet his, he loves her in a way that feels imperishable.

When he puts his hands over her breasts, she leans back and the wax flower falls to one side. 'We could scatter them,' she adds. 'If we had seeds,' her arms crossing at the back as if for yoga, to touch his thighs with opposite hands.

Only noises and chants, overtones and bells might really accompany what happens next. The butcher birds begin their song as up, up, Jeannie begins to move. Up, bravely up, she comes but also far enough away that he can see she is incarnadine, she could be French, she could be citrus in the rain and she is not moving her eyes from his that are also open.

The Favourite

Paul Mitchell

Before I see his face, I see his penis. In a cage behind rusted bars he's sitting on his haunches. Then he looks at me – or rather I lift my head and look at him. Though I have never before seen his face, I know he is the boy from my dreams. Under the house, on my knees, I stare at him and then I hear my mother calling. Through a gap in the weatherboards I see her in the garden carrying the tomahawk she uses for splitting our firewood.

But the boy doesn't exist. And he never will. What I give you is the fantasy of a seven-year-old girl that has become an old woman's memory. This old woman is now an unreliable witness, even to herself. She is a woman who mumbles in front of her friends as if she were asleep. She is someone for whom a bed with hard sheets is waiting a few blocks away. It's a bed not far from an activities room where someone will play piano. She will sit amongst men and women her age, with rugs across their knees, and listen to melodies that seem to come from a radiogram never permanently turned off in her mind.

He doesn't exist but her mother is real.

She smiles at her young daughter and asks her to help in the kitchen, to take the knives to the drawer and place them inside, quietly, because she doesn't like the clatter and racket. The young girl may lick the cake spoon – if she must – but not the inside of the bowl because that is a filthy habit, reserved only for those without manners and with no likelihood whatsoever of gaining any.

Her mother wears a floral apron, walks from bench to table, flour covering her arms; flour joined with water and the sun through a kitchen window so that her arms begin to flake. My mother's whole body turns white, flakes and collapses to the floor as I lick the spoon. I see her in pieces on the wood floor and then her face is in front of me, speaking.

'Why are you looking at me like that?'

'Sorry mother.'

'You should be, young lady.'

Only women visit our property and they talk with my mother in the sitting room. From where I sit in the library I hear muffled voices. One afternoon I enter to ask for a glass of water and my mother and another woman together on a settee move suddenly away from each other. Then the stranger goes back to signing papers on the mahogany table and my mother shouts me out of the room.

I meet him in a dream.

I am underwater and the women around me wear iron suits and upon their heads large yellow helmets with tubes extending from them and up towards the ocean's surface. I am as naked as when I get out of the copper tub at night, shaking droplets from my skin as my mother smiles and towels me. But she is not amongst the women underwater, the women whose mouths beneath their grills are saying that I must swim upwards, quickly, because I have no breathing apparatus, I am drowning. Behind them a large fish swims and then appears too suddenly before my face, eyes dark and bulbous. In that moment he swims past, too, yet I don't see his face. But I see his nakedness, the roundness of his buttocks, his calves scissor-kicking, the length of his arms stretching and bending.

He is older than me.

In a lace nightgown, I lift myself onto my elbows and breathe salty, midnight air on this our inland farm. The curtains beside the open window are motionless and there is a crescent moon and the sound of a dog somewhere, far away, barking.

The dog stops barking and it is my birthday. I am ten years old and my mother turns to me at the breakfast table and explains that I will not be going to school until I am thirteen, if I am even to go to school at that age. There is, for certain, no need for me to go to primary school. My mother says there has never been a need for anyone to go to primary school because teachers with their bad breath and canes are snide and she should know, she says, she should know. My mother watches the willow tree branches trying to push through a kitchen window and I nod at her, but she doesn't see. I go to my room and gather my hat and gloves because it is the day for our weekly two-hour shopping trip to town and I must be ready when Mr Forsyth arrives with the horse and cart for our silent journey.

I sit between Mr Forsyth and my mother and watch his large and gnarled hands grip the reins, but I make sure my mother doesn't see me looking. When we get to town men and boys are everywhere and my eyes widen until my mother stares down at me and prods me in the ribs with her index finger. I look at the ground, the footprints from large boots all up and down the red and orange dirt.

Between shops I take the risk and look up again. Men are talking on street corners, chins pointy under black hats, moustaches moving with smiles and laughter. I look at the hardness of the men's cheekbones and jaws and wonder what winds they have withstood to become so sharpened. They tip their hats at my mother and she ignores them as we pass. I hear muffled words and sometimes guffaws disguised to sound like coughs.

The one time I ask my mother where my father is she screams and cries for several hours and I can hear her no matter where I hide in the house or on the property, even the last gum tree at the fence line where our property borders the McTavish's. The next morning when she finds me she says my father died when I was a baby. You don't remember him, she tells me, though it was a dream about him that made me ask his whereabouts. But my mother says I must have been imagining things because I can't remember him. I hold her hand and walk inside.

My mother showed me photo albums when I was young, filled mainly with pictures of me, dressed in white lace or wool, bonnet tied under my chin. But on some pages there were four triangles set at the corners of a square, a square that should have held a photo, another building block for memory. But now I have only the memory of a photo's absence, keeping unsteady the memory of someone who doesn't exist. Who shouldn't exist. My mother quickly flicked past the pages with gaps and later, I'm sure, the gaps were filled with photos of me.

We're standing on a street corner and Mr Forsyth drives his cart towards us. As ever I have not seen my father amongst the men in town. But I have seen the boy. No longer naked, no longer underwater, he is in men's eyes, in voices gruffly calling out the price of fish or meat from market stalls. Mr Forsyth climbs down from the cart and pats his horses. My mother holds my hand and the boy is there in the way she does it. There in the warm fold of her hand itself.

Do you like the way it looks? It's real. Touch it.

There are always cake spoons to lick because my mother bakes relentlessly. Orange sponges, poppy seed, two-tiered hummingbird, black forest and caramel fudges. There are hedgehogs with sultanas as well as breadcrumbs, carrot cakes and fruitcakes and banana walnut loaves. Pikelets become my favourite but I do not tell her because previously I told her marble cake was my favourite and she stopped baking it.

Surely there are too many cakes for the two of us. Leftover slices are fed to the chickens and the occasional quarter cake, always cream, is in the rubbish pile. But the pikelets in the meatsafe; I know my mother doesn't like them. I haven't eaten them all, have I? I ask about them and soon, I recall, there are no more.

From the stairs late in the evening, I watch my mother knitting large garments. Some she lays on the hallway chest, coats for the horses to wear on winter nights. One night she carries to the door a smaller garment, freshly knitted, opens the door and returns without it.

I enter school and despite the gaps in my memory and education I also enter university because my mother assures me it is essential for a woman to have an exemplary education. At university I read Sigmund Freud and I think I understand that my life is partly an imagining. The boy has been a waking dream, a phantasm; the creation of an unconscious at war with a mother and indebted to a dead or missing father.

The lecturer stands tweed-suited at the front of the auditorium and continues the therapy which began when I was a young girl and the psychiatrist entered my room, the night the police brought me back from roaming in the night. The lectures concluded after several years and my mother died soon after they finished and then more therapy followed for me. Free association lying on a leather couch, afternoons of Rorschach drawings that seem now also to be dreams. Lectures, dreams or sessions, they all fill me now with the wish that I could believe everything I am telling is but a symbol, dragged from my unconscious because no one could possibly remember what I believe has happened.

It is in the asylum – how long ago? – that I first cry out.

He's real. Oh my Lord, he's real.

The exclamation is one among many, of mine and others'; a cry born from too much or not enough medication, bouncing off the white walls of the mid-twentieth century, raised from convulsive therapy or panic the nurses come to inject with soft dreams.

Don't tell her that you know. She'll kill me. You're imagining me … Can you do that?

I see him in dreams in the weeks before I meet him. Or are they dreams I had after I met him and he left my life? Or my life left me.

I am flying above clouds in a plane that doesn't have an outer casing, yet navy-uniformed and smiling hostesses I've seen in my mother's magazines parade the aisles, hairdos tightly bunned and secure under hats glued to their heads, their skirts not so much as rippling in the wind.

He is a voice speaking from where the cockpit of the plane should be. Then he is a cloud and then a pig in a pen that turns to his human shape, a muscled back, buttocks tight on his frame, but no face.

In the dream the plane never lands and the boy under the house is five years, I guess, maybe six years older than me.

My mother is coming with an iron axe. With teeth that burr with machinery.

Twenty-five, is it thirty years ago, I am reading Freud, or possibly Jung, in my cell over and over and the doctors walk past, no longer bothering to open the door and ask what I'm reading. I have discovered another universe and I slip my hands into it through the pages and pull them out covered in stars.

My mother hands me another spoon and I lick it.

My mother gives me a puppy. I lose it one afternoon while she bakes. I look up at her smiling face in the kitchen window. I search, below the window, push past the pittosporums and agapanthus that seem to be more and more flowers but then become a mural painted on the weatherboards. The mural has a door with an open padlock and later at university I read about the significance of locks in dreams.

I crouch down and enter the door, climb under the house, to the smell of rotting vegetables and cakes and I see a shape in a cage – a pig? – and I am not dreaming or speaking, I am not, and the pig makes no sound. He is there. Not in the eyes of any man in town or the memory of my father who I have never met. He is there.

Put your hand there … that's it, yes. Now rub …

The freight train stops at the station and the boy climbs on. In the darkness I make out the shape of his hand reaching for mine. I hold my hand out and though I can feel my body pushing my hand towards holding his, I don't grip it. I watch him in the carriage doorway, the train edging slowly down the track, his face visible for a moment under yellow light then gone. I wander away, aimlessly into the night, until I am picked up by the police and taken to mother, who smiles to have me back and holds me. At least this would be how things were if I had not read in university about what the unconscious is trying to say when it imagines trains and what it means to be taken home to mother rather than catching a train with my brother, who has escaped from my mother and from me and yet has taken me or my imaginings with him. Yet there is something of me that remains in the company of my mother.

The day after I meet him I still see his penis and his face and my mother's tomahawk and I am in the kitchen with her and she's baking a cinnamon bun, then it's on the table, wafting sugar heaven into the sunlight.

'Mother, do I have a brother?'

Her face turns to icing. White and candleless. Then she laughs and flushes.

'What kind of thing to say?'

I look at the fullness of her breasts, the round smile of her cheeks.

'I just wondered.'

I run to my room.

That feels good, just there. Now harder … Use your mouth now.

The police bring me back and the same night or the next night the psychiatrist is in my room, bowler hat and glasses. My mother says I cannot go downstairs, I must be in my bed where I can be monitored. The psychiatrist helps me with my imagination. Investigates it. Asks it questions. Tells me imagination is an interesting thing, but we cannot trust it. It must be trained, broken, like we train and break a horse, like my horse, Merrick.

'Do you remember when you first rode him? Did he buck? Yes? Your imagination is difficult to ride. But it can be broken.'

He goes with me into my imagination, then goes with me beneath the house. Or is under the house now in my room? There are empty cans and broken porcelain plates in the earth. Turned earth. Freshly turned, I'm sure. No mural. Pittosporums and agapanthus undisturbed in front of the weatherboards. Then we're standing beneath my mother's kitchen window and I can see her, hands in the sink and I can smell pikelets in the oven.

I am a witness to what is real. And what is imagination. And whatever exists between the two. A witness also to whatever a therapist believes or a mother denies or the dream about a brother foretells. I am an old woman ready to be taken this afternoon to where there are hard sheets and harder nurses. All their eyes are black, they will be, and I hear now a knocking on the door and then a key that opens it. My daughter enters, hair in a bun, the way my mother wore her hair when baking.

I am an old woman and I am unlocking him again and he is leaving his cage. I cry and tell him I am sorry for when I have played with him and that I could have unlocked him sooner if I had not enjoyed the playing and he is an old man and smiling and saying they were better than the games our mother played. Then he is a young boy and crying and running through wild flowers and a paddock in the night, past the gum trees, sentinels that line the fence and gate and I am running with him. I watch him running ahead of me, wearing my long pants; he is an 'itinerant worker', that is our ruse if we are questioned.

My mother isn't coming into this or any room to take me to hard sheets, she carries a cake spoon, she has lost her tomahawk and doesn't know where to find it. The policeman knocks on the door and she bends down and holds me and whispers, doesn't she, that they will never know and you will never know, either. And then she looks at me and hugs me again and says aloud, My lovely, beautiful boy. The policeman doesn't hear the slip. He must not have heard. He walks away and my mother scowls.

I lower my head to the pillowcase of my new bed and the lights go out and on again and photo albums fly in front of me, their pages turning. I see photographs of men in town, waiting on street corners, then one man, then a boy; photos float to the ground while the light flickers on and off; a boy, a man, an elderly man, asleep, hands folded and shut into a kitchen cupboard while my mother bakes.

What is your favourite, darling, what is it? I will make it for you.

Fuck Me Eyes

Amra Pajalic

When people ask me if I have any siblings I say, 'One, an older brother,' but that's not the truth. I have a sister, or at least I had a sister one summer years ago. The one thing I remember most about that summer is my sister's 'fuck me eyes'. Not that I knew what this meant, or that I would have thought of it as a description of my sister, but her 'fuck me eyes' were the reason she lived with us, and the reason she left.

It was when I overheard a friend of my brother's describe her as 'fuck me eyes, May' that I realised what her special quality was. I'd always accepted her flirting as an integral part of May. Some people measure their self-esteem by how many qualifications they collect or how many promotions they get; my sister measured hers by the barometer of how many men fell under her spell. She'd get all giggly as she talked about the checkout boy who gave her the once-over, or the bank teller who lingered over her notes while he made eye contact, but it wasn't until I heard the comment about her eyes that I started paying attention.

One day we were standing on the corner with the gang. If you knew my suburb you'd know there wasn't anything much to do other than hang around on street corners and shit-stir each other. We'd have to alternate corners because the neighbours in the corner house would get shitty and either threaten us with the hose or the cops, depending on how many kids they had. Mr Motopoulos had no kids living with him so he was the one who'd call the cops while Mrs Cloone had two sons, one fifteen and one thirteen years old, so she was the hose lady.

It was dusk and we were slapping and scratching our bare skin as the mosquitoes descended. My sister was wearing a spaghetti-strap top without a bra, denim cut-offs that barely covered her arse cheeks and had dangly strings of denim to her knees, and frilly ankle socks with high heels. Sounds weird doesn't it, frilly socks and high heels, yet somehow with her hair tied up with a scrunchy she had the unique look of the whorish-schoolgirl.

A car screeched up the street and the tyres squealed as the driver did a burnout. This was a regular occurrence in our street and didn't merit a look but as I was reaching to scratch my shoulderblade I caught sight of my sister. She was standing on the curb staring dead ahead at the driver who was speeding past us. I saw the moment she caught his eye, his head whipped toward her and their stares locked, then he drove past. Another squeal of the tyres and he did a U-turn, before pulling to a stop by us.

He spoke to one of the guys while staring at my sister. As I watched she looked down at the ground and quickly back up into the guy's eyes. With each drop of her eyes she moved and drew attention to another asset: a dip of her shoe in the street curb to show off her naked thigh and calf, a scratch of her shoulder which squeezed up her unfettered boobs. By dropping her eyes she gave the guy a chance to check her out yet each time she met his gaze again his attention was firmly back on her face. There was something about her eyes that drew them like bees to honey.

Before this I thought it had everything to do with the package, you know the tiny waist topped by Baywatch boobs. My sister was pretty close to the ground so even though her boobs were only a C-cup, on her petite frame they seemed like a D+. Her height had other advantages, apart from her boobs. I think there was something about her head never over-reaching a guy's armpit that made her so popular. That whole craning her neck to look up at the big guy seemed to make them feel manly, and being able to twirl her above their head with one arm, like The Incredible Hulk.

You're probably thinking this sounds a little like sour grapes and I guess you'd be right. Even though she was five years older, at twelve years of age I was already one centimetre taller than she was, and after that I gained one centimetre for each year of seniority she had on me. Hearing jokes about her in high school made me realise that being May wasn't so cool. Like the one that goes: 'first come the boobs around the corner and then ten minutes later appears May', or 'the advantage of having May as a girlfriend is you can use her breasts as a beer holder' or 'May doesn't complain about getting a crick in the neck from a blowjob since she can do it standing up'.

But that happened later. At this point, in the summer of my twelfth year, she was everything I wanted to be. We were polar opposites. I was tall, she was petite. I was blonde, she was a brunette. I had blue eyes, she had brown. I was fair-skinned, she had an olive tinge. The first few times we were asked about our lack of resemblance we told the truth and said we were half-sisters. When we received a blank look we had to go into the whole story: she was from our mum's first marriage, I was from her second, and we both took after our fathers. After a while we learned not to say anything at all – there were heaps of full-blooded siblings who shared no resemblance.

Watching May get into the car and disappear down the street with the guy made me burn with the righteous injustice only a pre-teen can feel as I looked from my bee-sting boobs to her udders. As I said, at this point I thought it had everything to do with the package and I believed that if only I grew huge boobs in puberty, my life would be perfect. Watching my brother's videos and seeing the porn actresses with huge boobs made me think that sex made boobs grow. So I'd started masturbating a few months earlier and was on the way to developing pretty extreme RSI in my right hand.

But when my sister came home that night and I opened our bedroom window for her I started to get an inkling of what her real attraction was. Her hair was out of the scrunchy and all messed up, her t-shirt torn slightly and there were hickey marks on her neck. She took off her t-shirt and denim shorts and I saw what looked like a snail trail on her tits and her belly. I watched as she rubbed it, her face dreamy.

'He loves me,' she said.

'Really?' I asked as I lay on my stomach on the bed. 'How do you know?'

'If you'd seen his face, you'd know it was true love,' she said before shrugging into her bathrobe and ducking into the shower.

After she went to bed I opened the drawer to my bedside table and stealthily pulled out my torch and book. Turning on the torch I opened the book to the marked pages. Re-reading the love scenes of the Mills and Boon, I slipped my hands into my underpants and fingered myself. The teasing passage and replayed images of my brother's porno fed my erotic fantasies. After I had an orgasm I returned the torch and the book. Remembering my brother's porno I saw again the looks of ecstasy on the men's faces as they came.

'May,' I called quietly. 'How do you know the difference between true love and sex?' I asked. Hearing no answer I turned over and went to sleep.

I was to find out over the next few days, as she waited for the call that never came, that she didn't. While we had dinner and then watched TV in the living room I could see that her ear was cocked for the phone to ring. Each time it did she was off like a greyhound bursting out of the cage, only for her face to drop when the caller asked for someone else in the family.

My father watched her antics with a wary eye. When she left the room for a minute he leaned over and said to me, 'I guess it won't be long before that's your dance?'

I giggled in delight. He sighed and shook his head, before leaning back in his armchair and switching the channel. Seeing my Daddy's face I sat on his knee and gave him a kiss and cuddle. He smiled, the worried frown fading. Hearing the living room door open I turned and saw that May had returned. She watched my father and I intently. I slipped off my father's knee and sat next to him to watch TV, avoiding May's eyes.

As we were getting ready for bed that night May slammed the bedroom door shut after she returned from brushing her teeth. I watched her warily as she shook the doona extra hard. She went to the vanity and put on her face cream. Hearing a crack, I jumped. She'd thrown the plastic tub against the mirror.

'Don't you think you're too old to sit on your daddy's knee?' she snapped holding my gaze in the mirror.

I left the room to brush my teeth. When I returned she was in bed and the light was turned off. I turned the light back on and saw my profile in the vanity. My boobs were lifting up the t-shirt slightly. I stuck out my chest trying to make more boob.

May had moved in with us six months before. Up until that summer she'd come to visit irregularly, maybe once a year. What I remember most about those visits is that my brother and I learned to sneak away from her. She'd come over to the house and then spend all her time helping Mum clean. If we weren't quick she'd rope us into cleaning our closets and putting away our toys. We used to be jealous because our mum would praise her for washing the dishes or folding the laundry while telling us off for messing up the living room with our toys. For months after May left she'd keep comparing us to her, 'If May were here' or 'May wouldn't do that.'

The year she moved in I'd twigged on to the value of having a sister. My brother, who was two years older, had moved onto high school and new friends, leaving me stranded in the band of pre-teen and soon-to-be-teen. With my sister I crossed over that line and learned about make-up, flirting and clothes. She was the one who noticed when my breasts had developed and took me shopping for my first bra. She didn't buy one of those crappy training bras that were made of nylon with the thin straps, but a flashy lace underwire bra that was the envy of my girlfriends. She was the one who taught me the value of good support in a bra in order to achieve great cleavage. She was also the one who bought me pads when I got my first period a few months before, told me about the dos and don'ts of tampons and what it meant to be a 'woman'. That was when I found out she was a virgin.

It was a Saturday and I had slept in. When I woke I was feeling sluggish, my lower back was aching and my legs were cramping. I ate breakfast in front of the tellie while catching the last half hour of *Video Hits*. During the commercial break I went to the toilet and found blood on my underwear. That's when I connected the sludge-coloured watery discharge of the past few months to my budding breasts. After padding my underwear with toilet paper I called May at her girlfriend's house and caught her before they left for the movies. Ten minutes later they dropped off the pads. When she came home that night we sat in the backyard behind the garage. She was smoking while I ate the leftover lollies she'd bought at the movies.

'So you know what this means, right?' she asked as she exhaled.

When I shook my head she sighed and blew her fringe out of her eyes. 'If you decide to fuck a boy you, my dear, can now get pregnant. Welcome to the joys of being a woman,' she said as she extinguished her cigarette on the brick garage wall and threw the butt under the fence where my parents wouldn't see it.

'So how come you're not pregnant?' I asked as I chewed the Red Skin I'd dug out of the lolly bag.

'Maybe because I haven't fucked anyone yet.'

My eyes smarted at her sharp tone. She'd never spoken to me like that before. I stopped chewing, the Red Skin sticking to my back teeth as I stared at the ground.

'And if I did I'd go on the pill so I don't get pregnant,' she said as she ran her hand through my hair.

After May left I overheard my mum telling a visitor that May had been thrown out by her father and stepmother because they found a packet of contraceptive pills hidden amongst her pads.

The visitor sipped her coffee and asked, 'What sort of a mother goes through her daughter's pads?'

My mum looked away without answering and wiped her tears. Even though she was May's biological mother, her stepmother had staked her claim as May's mum by rearing her from the age of five.

The weekend after my period was the first time May snuck out. When she called for me I opened the window to find her holding onto the fence for balance. As I pulled her through the window I smelled the alcohol on her breath. After taking off her clothes and putting her to bed I found smudged blood on her thigh and underwear. I went to the underwear drawer to get a pad and put it on her night table. Feeling foil under my hands I pulled out a pill packet and realised that it wasn't her period that was making her underwear bloody.

The next day I eagerly waited for her to wake up so I could ask her about 'it'. When she woke and saw her thigh, her face changed. When I saw her eyes my stomach went funny. It was like I wasn't looking at May. She looked at me as if she wanted to ask a question but couldn't remember what. I made an excuse and left the bedroom, avoiding her for the rest of the day. Her eyes changed after that. It was like she saw something that pushed her onto the outside and she couldn't ever find a way to return to who she was before 'it' happened.

When I came home from netball the next day my mum and dad were fighting. I'd just unlocked the front door and stepped into the hallway when I heard them in their bedroom.

'I don't like what she's doing to this family,' my dad said. 'I don't like the way she's changed everyone.'

I knew he was talking about me. May had taken me to get my ears pierced. When we came home Dad yelled at May and told her she had no right to get my ears pierced without asking permission. Mum jumped in and started yelling at Dad. I stood and watched, my ears burning while feeling like I was going to puke.

'Girls, go to your room,' my dad said, interrupting my mother's yelling.

I started walking off. Seeing that May wasn't behind me I turned around and saw she was staring at my dad without moving. I tugged on her arm and took her to the bedroom. After pushing her in I leaned my back against the closed door.

'Don't challenge me in front of the girls like that,' I heard my dad say through the closed door.

'Who the fuck is he to tell me what to do?' May said really loudly, almost like she wanted my dad to hear her.

I ran across the bedroom and slapped my hand across her mouth. 'Don't,' I begged as I started crying.

May took hold of my hand and pulled me into a hug. When we had dinner that night we all pretended that nothing had happened, but things were never the same after that.

' ... is growing up. It's natural for her to change,' I came back to the present when I heard Mum say my name.

'Yes, she is but it's as if she's abandoned her own family for May,' Dad sighed heavily. 'I don't like what's happening with us. We never used to fight like this.'

I remembered what life was like before May. My parents used to sit next to each other holding hands while we watched TV after dinner. Sometimes I'd catch them kissing each other on the lips, and by the look in their eyes I knew they were going to go to bed early.

'I know you feel guilty about leaving May, but she's not yours anymore. She hasn't been your daughter since she was five years old.'

'That's not true,' Mum said. 'All she needs is to be loved. She's never had that before. I wasn't there to love her.' I heard her crying. 'Please Doug, give it a little more time. Things will settle down.'

I went out the front door and closed it quietly. Counting to five I unlocked the door again and pushed it open with a bang. 'Anyone home?' I yelled.

Dad came out of my parents' bedroom. 'Hello,' he said, bending to give me a kiss. 'Are you hungry? There's some risotto on the stove.'

When May came home that night I tried to warn her. 'I

know your dad doesn't like me,' she said ruffling my hair. 'But it's OK, Mum's not going to let him do anything.'

I remembered the look in my mum's eyes at the dinner table as she glanced from Dad to May. She looked like the fox I saw on a doco who was being hunted by howling dogs but no matter how fast it ran, it wasn't fast enough. Ultimately there was only one way it was going to end for the fox.

Over the next couple of weeks my dad tightened the reins. He wanted to know where we were going and what we were doing every time we left the house. While I spoke, May stood beside me rolling her eyes or smacking her bubblegum.

I was sleeping on a Saturday night when I heard her moving around the room.

'May,' I called as I sat up in bed.

'Shhh, go back to sleep,' she whispered.

The curtains were pulled open and moonlight flooded the room, forcing me to close my eyes. When I opened them she was halfway out the window.

'May!' I yelped.

She froze, sitting on the ledge as we both waited. After a few moments we realised no one had heard. I pushed off my covers and crossed the room, grabbing hold of her arm. 'Come back. If my dad finds out you'll be in deep shit.'

She pried my fingers off her. 'I don't give a shit,' she whispered. 'It's like living in a Nazi camp. I want to have some fucken' fun.' Hearing a car she stopped and craned her neck. The car drove past. 'Let go of me. Rick's going to be here any second.'

Seeing her sitting on the ledge halfway to freedom I wanted to be her so badly. Just once I wanted to see what it was like to be admired and flirted with.

'Let me come with you,' I whispered.

She stopped and looked at me.

'Please,' I whispered, my voice high-pitched with excitement.

'OK,' she said returning to the room. 'But remember, you have to do exactly as I say.' She rifled through her dresser and grabbed some clothes before jumping out the window. I looked down at my nightie and hesitated in embarrassment. 'Come on,' she whispered impatiently. 'You can get dressed in the car.'

With one last look at my bedroom I jumped out the open window.

Rick took us to a nightclub where the bouncer was his friend. When we walked past the line and to the door Rick greeted him without introducing me or May. When we went to enter Rick's friend stopped us. 'Hold up,' he said to Rick. 'What is she, ten years old?'

'No,' May interrupted. 'She's eighteen years old. Show him your ID.' May nodded to me.

I flipped open my handbag and pulled out the learner licence May had borrowed from her girlfriend Rebecca. Both Rebecca and I had blonde hair – even though hers was dyed a platinum blonde and splitting at the ends – but that was the sum total of our resemblance. Rebecca had brown eyes and was twenty kilograms heavier than I was.

The bouncer looked from the licence to me. I looked away as per May's instructions. She'd told me I have a face that telegraphed guilt when I was lying. From the corner of my eye I saw the bouncer jerk his head for us to enter. I breathed out my relief and took back the licence.

It was my first time in a nightclub and the darkness took me by surprise. May and Rick walked ahead of me. She was wearing a white top and her customary denim shorts, frilly socks and stilettos. The white top and socks glowed under the strobe light. I walked behind them, my feet already aching from May's stilettos. I was wearing her clothes and we looked like twins, despite the lack of any resemblance. My hips hadn't developed yet so I just fit into her denim shorts.

May and I sat while Rick brought us drinks from the bar. I sipped through the straw and nearly choked. Rick winked at me. After doing the whole sickening smoochy thing with Rick while I pointedly looked away, May led me to the dance floor.

The dance floor revolved like a turntable. When I first stepped onto it I expected to be sick but it turned so slowly that if it wasn't for the changing faces who stood on the side, watching us, I would have forgotten it moved. We didn't even have a chance to start the lesbo moves that we'd practised at home because with each turn of the dance floor a guy would wave May over and we'd get off. She'd do the whole kissing on the cheeks thing and then they'd talk for a few minutes before she walked away. The conversation would be something like this:

'So cutie, are we going out tonight?' the guy would ask.

'You know I've got a boyfriend,' May answered.

'Oh, come on babe,' at this point he'd caress her arm, or her shoulder, or her cheek. 'Drop that loser and stay with me.'

She'd giggle and take the drink he was holding and slug back a few sips. Returning the drink she'd say 'You're so bad,' before returning to the dance floor, her booty shaking from side to side as the guy watched. Just before she reached the floor she'd turn and look over her shoulder, giving him a flirtatious look tinged with just enough hope so he'd keep trying.

The next time she stepped off I watched the other dancers. That's when I saw him. The guy who was going to be my first. He was wearing all white. This was the time of MC Hammer and the harem pants and this guy was a would-be-MC. He was doing the hip-hop moves among a crowd of admirers, mostly women, who jiggled from side to side in their version of a sexy dance. You know the step, shuffle, wiggle. He was ignoring all of them. You could see he was really into the music and almost unaware of everyone else around him.

The next time May stepped off, I moved away from her reaching hand and kept dancing. I kind of lost myself in the music. I was aware that May returned every few turns and tried to re-engage me in our lesbo moves but I ignored her and kept grooving to my own beat.

I don't know when I became aware that he had noticed me. All of a sudden I looked up and saw his little glance and felt this zing. You know the zing of knowing that a guy is attracted to you. We kept dancing and even though our bodies kept moving to the music, there was an awareness as we slowly moved toward each other. Everyone else was on the periphery and there was only the two of us and the chemistry as we grooved and bopped.

When we were standing in front of each other we kept dancing and slowly the distance between us disappeared. His hand was on my back, my hand on his shoulder. I looked up and met his eyes and we locked lips. I don't know how long the kiss lasted, it felt like forever and it felt like a second. There was no awkwardness or bumping of noses I had heard about from other girls at school. It was so easy, and so perfect.

Suddenly it was over. May's hard hand on my shoulder wrenched me away. I looked on in confusion as she turned on the guy and started shouting at him. 'What the fuck is wrong with you. She's only twelve years old!'

He looked at me and his face changed to disgust. He wrenched his arm from May and left. I watched his retreating back, the fluorescent white disappearing among the weaving bodies on the dance floor. May was talking to me but I didn't hear her. When I came back to earth I realised she was asking if I was OK. 'Did he do anything to you?' she asked, peering into my face. Her mouth smelled of alcohol and her speech was slurred.

I pushed her away and ran. She found me an hour later in the toilet cubicle. When I came out she wanted to say something but I cut her off. 'I want to go home.'

She tried brushing my hair away from my face but I jerked away from her touch. 'Well maybe in an hour. Rick is with his friends and – '

'I want to go home now,' I shouted in her face.

For a minute, she seemed hurt, but she quickly rallied and stood in front of the mirror. She rifled through her purse and found her lipstick. 'I don't know why you have to be such a scaredy baby,' she said as she applied her lipstick.

I moved to stand behind her. 'Either we go home now or I'll call my dad.'

She met my eyes and looked away. 'OK, we're going home,' she said as she threw her lipstick back in her handbag.

I saw that her lip-line was crooked but I didn't say anything as I followed her to find Rick. I stood back as she spoke to him. She leaned down and almost sat in his lap as she whispered in his ear. He got up a minute later and walked with her under his arm to the car park.

When we reached his car he pushed May against it and started kissing and grinding himself against her. 'What are you looking at twerp?' he said scowling at me. He unlocked the back car door and held it open. 'Go back inside, kid,' he said as he pushed May in. As he went to follow May into the back-seat he said with a grin, 'Unless you want to join us.'

'I want to go home,' I said, my voice high and panicky.

'Yeah, well, I'm not ready. So fuck off,' he said, taking a step toward me like he wanted to hit me.

I took a step back. 'May, come on. Let's go home.' I held out my hand to her.

She was sitting on the edge of the car seat, her eyes jumping from me to Rick. 'No. I'm having fun,' she said, looking away from me.

'May, come on, I'm scared – '

I didn't see Rick move until I was on the ground. He'd pushed me, the unexpected force propelling me until I lost my footing and fell to the ground awkwardly. My palms stung and I'd scraped my knee. Seeing his feet as he approached me I screamed as he lifted me up by the shoulders and pushed me again, with less force this time. 'Fuck off kid.'

I stumbled toward the club, my eyes blurry as I cried.

'I won't be long and then we can go home,' May shouted behind me.

I didn't turn around. The car door slammed shut as I continued walking to the payphone in the club foyer.

Object Lessons

Alison Ravenscroft

1. The doll

Do you remember the smell of a doll's plastic body and the pinkness and the hardness of the doll against your belly as you pressed yourself close to it for the comfort? Or were you the kind of girl who refused the doll, fearing its mix of the living and the dead?

When a mother first gives her girl a doll, she thinks only of the innocence of the thing: its tiny body and big eyes. She does not remember a doll's perversions. For all dolls have their darker side, the side that requires the child to punish the perfect passive body. A Barbie doll carries something in her body that is unbearable to small girls, she stirs something in them. They dress her and undress her, they press her arched feet into her shoes, they fondle and tear at the perfect hair. At dusk, they take her down to the water's edge. They do not hear their mother calling them into the light of the little fibro holiday house, calling them into the warmth. They do not see their mother standing behind them, her long evening shadow mingling with theirs in the waters. They are entirely preoccupied with the acts they are performing on their seven Barbie dolls, dressing each one in a costume of fantastic design and lying them face down in the shallows, where they move slowly in the waters. There are seven drowned Barbies, long hair, satin and sequined tulle floating around their hard little bodies. Don't ever imagine there is tenderness in a girl for Barbie. Barbie is never loved, merely coveted. When all the dolls are dressed and drowned the two small girls see the mother's shadow and in a single move they turn up their faces towards her and smile, beatifically.

Some girls love their dolls, cherish them, find comfort and companionship in their stillness. There is Baby Doll in her handmade satin dress with rough lace trim, and her tiny cardigans, knitted in clumsy uneven rows by a mother and grandmother sitting in their kitchen on the night before Christmas. The old woman is not fond of dolls. Her own doll stands on top of the cistern with her legs inside a toilet roll, her purple crocheted skirt over the roll like a crinoline, a startled look on her face.

For the young girl, Baby Doll lives, her body is flesh. She is beauty, perfect and complete. Only when time passes and the girl grows older does she see Baby Doll's broken eye and matted hair, her shabby dress. Then, Baby Doll returns to the status of a thing, she takes on the condition of the unloved. She can no longer breathe, or feel, or remember. Yet there hovers all around her the memory of what she used to be, the powers she once held, when the girl loved her.

2. The mother's hands

The mother is wrapping the old dolls between sheets of tissue paper in a little cardboard box. As she holds each doll and tucks it between the folds of paper, pressing one doll gently against another so that no doll should feel cold or alone, she is holding the past in her hands. In the materiality of the object, the past and all its longings are brought into the palm of the hand and grasped there. The mother is holding her own small daughter again, the girl now grown away.

This mother's hands are hands that love, even when the body to which they belong pushes away from another's touch. They are big hands that make babies secure in their hold, that can span nine keys on the piano, they are hands that, whitened with flour, leave soft marks around the kitchen. They are hands that are frequently burnt, knocked against the hot trays of the oven by a woman who is hurried and wishes the baking done; a woman who comes to the table with butter on the burns and something gripping her stomach so that she no longer wants to eat. She sits on the edge of her chair, poised as if for flight, sipping a sherry to soothe her but which only loosens the hold of her self-control, so that she starts singing old music-hall ditties, flirting with her husband, wanting something from him he will never give.

And those who love her will eat her disappointment.

3. The Singer

The grandmother was used to working with needle and thread, sewing together scraps of satin and lace. She had been a seamstress since she was a girl and she was still working when she was seventy, bowed over an ugly electric sewing machine, feeding the fabric towards the menace of the needle. She knew the feel of satin and lace as it slid under fast hands, turning scraps of fabric into a pretty petticoat or chemise. At home there were always materials she had picked up cheap, the last of a bolt of pale blue gingham, a couple of yards of machine-lace from a discontinued line. She would take up these remnants with love, and on her treadle make delicate things, slowly now. For the treadle was not the machine of her bondage. She loved its delicate wrought-iron frame and the little drawer where the reels of cotton were kept amidst the tangle of a tape measure. But most of all she loved the silver paint which spelt out the machine's name – SINGER.

They came with so little – her husband's bicycle, one small trunk, and the sewing machine. When, with her small broken feet, she would press a rhythm out of the treadle, it was as if she had set the machine to singing and was listening for the traces of an old song that might carry her back to that other time and place. *It was and it will never be again.*

4. Tutu

Do you know the touch and smell of ballet shoes, their supple pink leather and straining satin? Do you know the feel of a bound foot and a tutu's stiff upturned hem?

The young girls learn to open their bodies, arching them so as to expose heart and throat, leaning into the positions of surrender. The ballet teacher takes a girl's small foot in her hands and shapes it into a point until it mimes those moments of pleasure when the feet arch themselves in ecstasy. The mothers come to watch their daughters learning the dance, and their throats grow full and tight. They mistake their pleasure for motherlove. As the class comes to a close, the teacher beats out a polka from the old piano and the girls swing each other in wide circles, finding something in the polka's rhythm that brings out the wildness in their little bodies. The mothers move closer, encircle the girls, touch their heat and urge them into quietness.

5. Bone china

Do you remember the way your mother held her teacup, cradling it in both hands for its heat? Do you have that cup still, drink from it, press its rim against your lips as once your mother pressed it against her own, a kiss which might cross the impossible time and space of your loss?

One day, or so the promise went, her mother's tea-set would come to her. But china is a fragile thing. It carries the passage of time as a gap, or a wound. In clumsy hands a cup is dropped, a fracture appears in another, dark blooms fade under milky glaze distressed by overuse. When the time came, one teacup remained. It was sweet and perfect and, by its very solitude, marked all the missing parts. For this teacup will always belong to a set, however broken or dispersed are its parts.

6. The grandfather clock

When her grandfather died, a long wooden box arrived and was laid on the lounge-room floor. Its lid was prised open and the small girl thought: Grandpa is in there. But it was not a man's body after all, but the body of a great clock, and it seemed no less human for that. Her father moved its huge mass upright and leant it against a wall, inserted the key and wound up the mechanism, set the pendulum into motion, and gently moved the clock's ancient hands to the correct time.

But the clock would not go, it would not take its own breath or keep up the rhythm of its own heart. It needed coaxing, her father faithfully setting and re-setting the pendulum, moving the hands again so they might briefly indicate the time of day. *Re-commence your eternal round, and make a home for me in this bloody empty land.* The clock's malady stood not only for his lost father but for all that had been left behind. And then the clock started up, and kept going without a day's rest for forty years, until his thoughts turned to leaving.

The clock is over two hundred years old, her father said, *keeping time before Cook came to this place.* The time this clock kept was not restricted to the hours of a single day but spanned all the hours and the days that made up two centuries. It didn't merely measure time but faithfully recorded it. It was as if the clock's mechanism, instead of driving hands around a face, had pushed a nib across the surface of its wooden casing and inscribed there all the events that made up its days. To her father, that clock was a book, its pages made of wood and ancestors' skin, its ink was time and the blood that binds.

The clock stood eight feet tall and the striations in the rose-wood were like ribs in a man's chest. The young girl used to kiss the wood, kiss it in that wet, open-mouthed way children have. When her father left, he took the clock. He made a wooden box for it and when the time came for the box to be closed, his daughter kissed the clock's belly. She cried more for that clock's going than she did for her father's. It was not that she loved the clock more, but wood vibrates with the past in a way that flesh and blood cannot. As the flesh begins to vibrate with the past it becomes weary and passes away. The past is carried in less mortal things: in a teacup or an old clock, in a scrap of pink tulle and some spools of thread.

On the Yarra Glen to Yea Road

Sue Robertson

The cool change came through shortly after six in the morning. Don't ask me why that's important, or even why I remember it, since it has absolutely no bearing on what happened that day. Or why we are here today.

We had stopped at a roadhouse halfway between Yarra Glen and Yea on the Melba Highway. You'd know it. You travel that way yourself, I've seen you. It's about five or six kilometres on from where the Toolangi Forest runs out and the farmland starts. There's a little house there, right under the high voltage wires, that brings to mind that scene from the movie *The Castle.* You can feel the serenity scene with Michael Caton and that girl out of *Always Greener.* The traffic on that particular section of road must be horrendous in the ski season.

The roadhouse is right there, just beyond the Glenburn pub where the road does a big sweep to the right. Driving that way it's wise to slow down. It's a sixty zone and the country cops sit in front of the fire brigade shed and wait.

They make the best chips at that roadhouse. Not that on that particular morning we'd stopped for chips, or the egg and bacon sandwiches the interstate truckies stand in line for. We'd stopped for petrol and a wee.

That's when the change came through. A south-westerly that flew over the range and hit that part of the Upper Yarra

Valley with a splintering force. It brought the rain and then a shock of hailstones like bullets.

Being January, it caught everyone off guard. The A-frame advertising board on the verge flew across the road. The '98 cents a litre Unleaded' hoarding was almost horizontal. Hank said 'fuck' because we had to make a real run for it across the bitumen to the car. We didn't want to get saturated but it was impossible to avoid it. I was just grateful we weren't lugging buckets of chips. We'd have lost them for sure.

The rain and the hail stopped as quick as it'd started, but it left us wrapped in the gloomiest atmosphere I could ever recall. It was like being inside a shroud. The sky wasn't black and it wasn't grey, it was a mouldy, dirty green. Had we been further up the road nearer the mountains, I'd have said there was snow on the way for sure.

With our petrol tank full and our bladders empty, we left the roadhouse with its bains-marie full of the best chips this side of Port Douglas, the egg and bacon sandwiches, the hamburgers, and the jars of homemade berry jam stacked on shelves by the door, and we pulled onto the road. The radio was just starting to get the jitters. We'd missed the six o'clock news and Hank said we'd have to wait until seven to find out what the weather'd be. My guess was it'd be bleak and cold like it was now but he was in no mood to be humoured so I sat tight-lipped and watched the passing parade.

There wasn't much. A few tankers and a caravan, all heading the other way. There's very little of significance at six o'clock on a Sunday morning on the Yarra Glen to Yea road. There are goats and alpacas in the closest paddocks. And olive trees. Pretty trendy here, but not as trendy as further back down the valley where it looks more like Tuscany than Tuscany. Good wine though. And olive oil. My nan, Mum's mum, was born in Italy. Not in Tuscany though, further south than that. It was my plan to go there, one day. Take Nan back to where she came from.

With the radio off, and the car still being hammered by the wind, I thought to point out the three-armed spiked windmills on the hills, since Hank was interested in alternative energy and just recently I'd heard a fellow from Goughs Bay talking about these windmills. There are a lot around Warrnambool and Port Fairy, and people are always getting their knickers in a knot over them. Strange thing is, everyone wants alternative energy but no one wants it coming from anywhere near them. It's like airports, I suppose. Hank could be quite vocal on the subject but that wasn't the case on that particular morning.

Hank didn't want to talk about much at all but then Hank wasn't much of a talker at the best of times. His thing's photography. I'm a model. A photographer's model. And we were on our way to Sydney to take photos in the city parks up there. It was going to be a series. We planned to travel to parks all over the country and at sunrise and sunset I'd hang from trees in artistic poses. Suited me. I'm athletic. I did gymnastics at school and would have got into the state team if I hadn't fallen off the balance beam and broken my ankle when I was eleven. Even before that, Dad wanted me to be a tennis player and Mum wanted me to be a ballet dancer. My forehand was good, but my backhand was shite. And I got bunions from the toe shoes in ballet. Gymnastics was always my first love anyway, and, even with my ankle, it proved pretty useful when I was posing for Hank.

I have long black hair – long to my waist. Hank said I look great in the nude. I think so too. See how my hair flips when I shake my head. It looks fantastic when I'm upside down. It's like a shiny black waterfall. At least that's how Hank liked to describe it. I don't think we should be ashamed of our bodies. It's only nature after all.

Hank said this series would make his name, like Mapplethorpe's *Orchids*, he said. Imagine me – in one of those big glossy books on coffee tables in South Yarra or Noosa. Noosa's the new South Yarra, Hank said. And if it makes his name, it will make my name, because I'm his muse, like Elle MacPherson was to Norman Lindsay in that movie with Sam Neill.

It can be uncomfortable hanging around like a bat for hours but it's worth it in the end. Hank's taken some sensational shots. Not that I could ever show my mum though, art or not, according to her views, no daughter of hers should be seen in her birthday suit, in public, at least not after the age of two years.

We were at that part of the road where the ranges on both sides sort of split and the wind really whips through. It was snapping at Hank's car. He was really pissed off. I could tell from the set of his mouth. His car's a clapped-out Hillman Imp, in a murky yellow colour. But you'd know that already. You saw it. Maybe if you hadn't been having such a good look, you wouldn't be here. Maybe I wouldn't be here either. But that's history now.

That was the first thing Hank was going to buy when he made it big as a photographer – a new car. Nothing flashy like yours. Hank's not the flashy type, but it wouldn't have been too shabby either. It certainly would never have been a Hillman Imp. Or a Cortina. Hank always said only old people drive Cortinas.

We wanted to be in Yea by daybreak but we'd sort of tied one on the night before so we slept in, and then with that wind going straight across the road it was going to take even longer. That was what was making Hank so testy. There's a fantastic park in Yea. It's a nature reserve with all kinds of birds and stuff, and reeds and old bent boughs that dangle into the lake. There's one particular tree that Hank just loved. He could get practically orgasmic about it, but the trouble is it's quite near to the road. The cops park in the driveway of the park with their cameras out the window. The last time we were there I told Hank they were only interested in the cars on the road, not the naked girl hanging from the tree, but he never even cracked a smile. That was how seriously Hank took his work. Getting his shot and making his name was all that mattered to him, I swear.

We wanted that tree-shot for our daybreak series. We saw it as being the main piece of the series but we wouldn't be getting it that day. Even if we'd got there earlier, it was never going to work out, not the way Hank wanted it to. I did mention before that Hank was a perfectionist, didn't I? He still wanted to take the photograph though. I wasn't so keen. It felt like it was getting colder, and Hank wasn't the fastest shot. Still, I'd posed in worse weather, and we both reckoned it'd be worth it. And it would have been if Hank had taken that bend a little more slowly. The cops said it was the brakes, so it wasn't his fault.

That's when I saw you in your flashy bluc car. What is it? A Volvo. A Lexus – really? It must have been a very smooth ride. I didn't see another car for an hour and a half after you went by. I thought you'd send someone back to help us. I waited. Hank was so still, just whimpering from time to time. I was starving. I kept thinking of the chips at the roadhouse, wishing we'd bought some.

That's my mum down there, in the black skirt and floral top. Do you see her? Second from the end in the third row from the front. She's come today with my sister. She looks a lot like me, don't you think. People used to say we could've been twins.

My mum's like a groupie. She's at all these things. Not that I blame her – the only thing I find strange is that she has so many questions now when she wasn't the least interested when I could answer them in person. I suppose a lot of them here today are like that.

You're uncomfortable, I can see. Probably watched those shows on television and thought what are these people doing thinking this guy in the black skivvy can communicate with their loved ones. I did too. I'll tell you what changed my thinking, it was that couple over there. Like me and Hank, they were just doing their own thing when it happened, except instead of driving along the road to a great park, they were rafting down a river in Switzerland. On their honeymoon, which, in my view, makes it ten times worse, when they got caught in a flood. It was in all the papers.

The last time I was here I heard him tell her parents that their daughter and her new husband were still together and that no one should be blamed. That it was an accident. Her parents went away looking so peaceful, and that's when it clicked with me. Before that I was as much a sceptic as you are now but when I saw that look on those people's faces I thought, that's what I want for my mum. It's such a little thing for us to do, but it means the world to them.

Having spent this time with you, I find I like you. That's the way it is here. When I first saw you flash past in your shiny car, staring through the window at Hank and me in that crappy old car smashed against that tree trunk, my thoughts weren't kind. And as time went on and no help arrived, I really have to say I despised you, but that's only proof none of us should judge. And that's why I am comfortable enough to ask you this. I need for you to be me – just this one time – for my mum and sister, I mean. There are so many of us here today, and so many there. You really will have to be pushy to break through all the noise. Start with my initial – if you do it right he'll ask if the initial E or P or something means anything to anyone in the audience. Watch their faces – they'll be desperate for it to be them, even the sceptics. No one made them come here today – they might pretend they came under duress, but no one comes to an event like this if they don't want to. Keep prodding at him. A young girl – long black hair – passed suddenly. Watch. The faces will fade from desperation to polite interest. Only one or two will make a connection. Then you go into the specifics. I've made a list. If you still don't get a response, prompt her with the name Bingle. You just say 'Bingle', and he'll say – does the name Bingle mean anything to anyone? Bingle, a black and white cocker spaniel? After that you should be home and hosed. Bingle is hardly a common name for a cocker.

Once you're through, there's no need to say much. They don't want to know much. Keep it simple. Tell her I'm with Nan. She'll like that. They don't seem to understand how big this place is. Truth is, I could search for years and never find Nan. I did hear she was out west, happy as a lark. Can you tell her I am happy? That's what she needs to know the most. It's what all of them are here for. The trick is to be patient, and to be subtle. It's the little things that give them peace of mind. It'll be good practice for you, for when your family finally does come. Although, even when they do come, don't expect them to jump in straightaway, some of them have to come several times before they are comfortable enough to listen.

I'd do it myself, of course I would, but Hank's in a bad place, but so's his dad; Hank doesn't seem to get that. His dad is so depressed and so desperate for answers he's booked a one-on-one, and that can't have been easy for him. Matter-of-fact, he's across town right now but Hank refuses to be there. Says he isn't ready to talk to his father yet. Truth is he's angry. He blames his father for a lot of things that went wrong for him and his mum when he was growing up. But someone should be there. The way I figure it, I was Hank's muse, so it's my responsibility. I know enough to give the old man the answers he needs for now, and maybe next time Hank can talk for himself.

The Passport

Janey Runci

My little barbarian. That's what she called me. Barbarina, sometimes, or Little Barbara, as if I were a doll. Barbara is my second name, my mother's name. Colette saw it on my passport.

We were in Vienna when Colette called me her little barbarian. I asked her some question, some innocent question about the carvings in St Stephen's Church and she laughed. She had tears in her eyes from laughing. I moved away from her, down the side aisle. I had to push past a group of people, local people I think, kneeling at a small shrine at the side. I had tears in my own eyes by then, but I wasn't laughing. The people praying swayed a little as they whispered their words in a singsong rhythm. An old woman looked up at me, frowned and crossed herself, but then shuffled along the kneeler, gesturing for me to kneel beside her. She bent her head and kissed what I saw was the cross of her rosary beads.

I knelt beside her, crossed myself awkwardly. There was a spicy smell from the woman, not quite cinnamon, but rich, like a soup. I reached for my handkerchief to wipe my eyes and my hand brushed against her green cape. The material was surprisingly soft.

On my other side a large man with a grey moustache prayed in a growling monotone, dipping his head regularly. I was beginning to recognise the parts of the prayers, the Hail

Marys, the dipping of the head for the name of Jesus. My own lips began to move, although I didn't speak the language. I was like a child again, between my parents, pretending to know the words of the prayers. Candles flared and sputtered in a brass holder in front of our kneeler.

Barbarian. Colette would be wondering where I was. She wouldn't be able to see where I'd knelt down. I almost got up, but then I decided to stay. I imagined her looking for me, still laughing but gradually getting worried. She might even ask someone, a guide, or another tourist. She'd ask if they'd seen a young tourist in jeans and a red jacket. She'd try to speak casually, or what she considered to be casual. She would never believe that she sounded imperious when she spoke English.

'Young man,' she would call to a waiter in a restaurant in her British actress voice. She'd learnt English by listening to BBC radio, when she first arrived in London in 1940, eighteen years old, the only one of her family to get out of Vienna early enough. She'd listen to the radio, trying to repeat words. I imagined her brown eyes intent, her lips moving in time to the words.

The rhythm of the rosary was soothing as I knelt there in St Stephen's Church. To my right, at the back of the church I saw a group of tourists being shepherded out by a guide holding a small flag above his head and then I saw Colette approach him. She stood as she always did when she was asking for information, her head tipped back, her eyes looking down at the person she was questioning. That day she'd worn her Jag jacket. 'Good cut and style is timeless,' she'd told me when she put it on.

The Jag jacket had a tiny check in sage green and from where I was kneeling Colette did look stylish, almost sculptured. The guide was shaking his head and looking round, probably for the last of his group. He tried to move past Colette, but she held him there. He shook his head again and then pushed past her with his small flag bobbing above the heads of the group who filed out of the church.

Colette was on her own then, a tiny figure at the base of the soaring dark walls of the church. Her head was moving from side to side as if she was studying the walls, the paintings and carvings, but I knew her eyes would be glittering with anxiety. I watched her for a moment, pretending to pray, and then I pushed myself up and went to join her.

*

The Milan railway station was full of echoes. All the voices, the voices of the people like us down on the platforms and in the concourse area, the voices of the loudspeakers announcing the trains, all these voices seemed to be floating in spools of soundtrack somewhere under the glass-domed roof. I kept looking up. Whenever we came near to a door another soundtrack joined us, the sound of the traffic outside. We were pushed and jostled as we trundled our cases along.

'Be careful to stay together,' Colette said.

We had to go slowly for Colette to manage her case which was almost twice the size of mine.

'What if I go ahead and check the platform?'

'There's no need,' Colette said. 'We've got plenty of time.' She stopped, clearly out of breath and pulled out the wallet with the passports and tickets. She leafed through them, as though she needed to check them, but she'd done this three times before we'd left the pensione that morning. Once again I was tempted to ask for my own passport and ticket back, and once again I didn't. It had all happened so smoothly, so unobtrusively. 'Can I have a look at your ticket and passport?' she'd said. 'I want to check something.'

I couldn't imagine what she wanted to check but it didn't seem to matter and I handed them over willingly enough. I'd been propped at the window of our pensione, watching the Milanese setting off for work. Businessmen swinging into the small tram that wound its way up the street, elegant girls who I imagined were sales assistants for the various boutiques that lined the street walking together in pairs and chatting, going into the bars for their morning coffee. I could see all this through the bare branches of the trees that lined the street. It was late winter but the air was warm with a hint of spring. It was only later when we were leaving the pensione that I asked Colette for the passport and ticket. I was bent over my case, unzipping the pocket where I kept my travel documents. I looked up, expecting to see Colette handing me the papers, but she was standing in front of the mirror, her lips spread thin as she applied her lipstick. I waited until she finished, still expecting the papers, but she just dropped the lipstick into her handbag, snapped the clasp shut.

'They're safer together,' she said. 'And besides, I've already packed them away.'

I stared at her bag. She'd shown me the zipped pocket inside for her papers. It would be no trouble for her to open it and take mine out, but she had already swung it over her shoulder and she was edging her suitcase to the door.

'I'm going to call for that porter,' she said. 'But remember, no tipping. His service has been quite unsatisfactory.'

Once again the woman who ran the pensione would stand at the door of the small room off the dining room where her husband dozed in front of the television and yell at him to come and help. He would come out blinking, his shirt untucked, disturbed from his sleep. He had a job in the city in the afternoons. I was going to give him a tip. At least I still had my own money.

*

When we were out on the street it didn't seem to matter so much about the papers. I was in Milan, it was almost spring. The wheels of our cases rumbled cheerfully over the stone paving.

'Ah, Milano,' I said to Colette in my new Italian accent and she laughed. Today we would leave for Bologna. Milano, Bologna. I was really here.

Colette stopped me in front of a shop window with bags arranged in box cubes hanging by wires from the ceiling. In each box was one bag. Colette pointed.

'That one would suit you.'

I saw first a red bag with a large silver buckle on the side. It was the kind of bag I would have loved when I was a little girl, but I knew Colette wouldn't be meaning this one. I could see another one, a sage green one, and it was beautiful, but it was a real handbag, the kind my mother would have given anything to own, the kind that would be owned by a woman who wore Jag jackets. I shook my head.

'Not my style,' I said.

'It could be,' Colette said. She looked at me and then back at the window. 'If you'd only let me I could make you look stunning.'

I held my breath, stared straight ahead.

'Why don't we go in and have a look?' she said. She looked at her watch. 'We've got enough time.'

I shrugged, tried to look casual. 'I'd rather go and have a coffee.'

'We can do that too. Come on, let's go in.' Her eyes were soft now and eager. 'I was going to surprise you, but I'll have to tell you now. I want to get you something, something special to remember the trip by.'

'But these bags are so expensive.'

'I know. And I know you don't like the green one. That's not the one I meant.'

'Which one then?'

Colette pointed up to the box on the left. The bag was made of a soft black material. It was being held in the cube by a cord of some kind so that you could see it went over one shoulder and across the body. I imagined it resting on my hip. I ran my hand over my hip.

'See?' Colette said. She was looking at me and smiling.

The woman in the shop showed us that the bag had a special pocket inside for travel papers. I almost asked Colette for the papers then, I thought she might even offer them to me, but she didn't and it seemed childish to insist.

The bag went perfectly on my hip. It fitted easily and softly across my breasts and it was so easy to get out my money when we came to get the coffee. Every now and then as we sipped the coffee I found myself running my fingers over the smooth satiny feel of the bag. I'd never had a bag quite like this, never thought there could be such a bag, one that looked so elegant, but was still practical.

*

While we waited to pick up the seat allocations at Milan station I thought again of asking for my papers. I could just pick them up after the clerk inspected them, but there was a problem with the bookings. The clerk claimed we'd never booked. I had enough Italian to explain that we'd booked when we left Vienna, but the clerk just shook his head. Then Colette stepped forward, spoke to him in German, and suddenly he responded in German. They argued loudly for a minute or so and then the clerk finally printed out the seat numbers, shaking his head all the time and muttering. Colette stood in front of me, sliding the tickets and passports and seat numbers back into her travel wallet and into her handbag. The clasp snapped shut. She pushed back from the counter with a grand and angry wave at the muttering clerk.

*

The train for Bologna was a long way down the platform.

'We should get some water and food,' I said.

'No. We'll find our carriage first.'

Colette was pale by the time we found our seats. She leant back in the seat and closed her eyes.

'I'll go back and get the water,' I said. 'And a panini?'

Walking back down the station it struck me that this was the first time I'd been without some kind of heavy bag or case for some days. Only my new bag on my hip, soft and light. I strode out. On this part of the platform there were gaps between the sections of roof and I felt the warmth of the midday sun on my head and shoulders. I was in Milan station, I was going to Bologna. I wanted to run. I did run. I ran down to the sandwich bar at the end of the platform, but there was a crowd there. Now that I was unburdened I could probably make it back to the trattoria that had the special panini we loved.

The woman who served me the panini pointed at my bag. 'Bellissima,' she said. I smiled back and nodded. Outside I stopped at a newsstand and bought two Italian magazines. I could see the grand opening out into the streets of Milan and for a moment as I waited I had a desire to walk straight out of the station and into the streets, to be lost in the crowd, never to return to my case, and Colette and her huge case.

'Signorina?' the man behind the counter said as he handed me the change.

Platform Thirteen seemed to be further back than I remembered. I could see the train further down, but then I read the sign. Venezia. I stood for a moment studying the board. Thirteen A. I had to go back.

I jogged a bit as I got to the right platform. I was getting hot, especially when I went under the open parts of the roof. Up ahead the train seemed to be shimmering. I would be glad to sink into the upholstered seat. An announcement came over the speakers and I began running, but nothing more happened. People still stood round the doors of the train further up the platform. I walked for a little bit, taking deep breaths and as I began running again the train slipped slowly away from me. It just seemed to glide. I ran faster, came level with it, got to the last door and a man who had been waving goodbye to friends on the platform leant down and somehow pulled and levered me onto the step and then into the corridor of the train. I leant against the wall of the corridor, breathing hard.

'Oh, signorina, signorina,' the man kept saying.

'Grazie, grazie,' I said. I pointed further down the corridor, trying to let him know that I had to get to another carriage, but he seemed to understand.

When I had my breath and my legs felt strong enough I began to make my way down the swaying carriage. I was already rehearsing the story for Colette. It just seemed to slide out ... completely silent ... no announcements ... you should have seen me running ... and I was saved by the most gorgeous Italian man. The man was dark, I remembered, and smooth-shaven. He smelled of a beautiful cologne. I was right up against him. Right up against his groin, in fact, but I hadn't felt anything because the black bag had swung around. It had been embarrassing, the buckle of the bag getting caught in his trousers, and he'd had to unhitch it while I stood there, but he'd been charming throughout.

'Where have you been?'

It was Colette, swaying from side to side as she came down the corridor beside the windows of the carriage. Her face was even paler than before. 'I didn't know where you were.' She was almost spitting. 'I was out of my mind with worry. I've told you so many times about being on the train on time.'

'Look.' I held up the panini and magazines.

'What if you'd missed it? I had the passports and the tickets. You would have been in a sorry mess.'

She closed her eyes, clenched her fists and then swung around and began to make her way back to our carriage. Even while she swayed her neck was rigid with anger as I followed behind. When we got to our compartment she pushed roughly past the knees of the other passengers. Earlier she'd made a fuss of giving me the window seat because it was my first time going to Bologna, but now she flung herself down in that seat, pressed her face against the window so that she had her back to me. I smiled apologetically at the others as I lowered myself into the seat.

I sat there beside Colette's back, thinking about my passport. I wanted to yell at her. That's exactly the problem, I wanted to yell. I don't have my passport, or my ticket. Then I tried to calm myself, took deep breaths, imagined speaking calmly, politely. Perhaps I should have my passport and ticket. I imagined slipping the passport into my new bag.

Gradually Colette sunk a bit further in the seat, her head resting against the side cushion. I thought she might be falling asleep. Past her shoulder I watched the grassy patches on the banks beside the railway line. I saw a flash of red and then another and suddenly I realised they were red poppies, red poppies growing wild. I leant forward to see and then I went into the corridor. A man opened a window for me. I leant out, breathing in the sooty air. I saw banks and banks of red poppies in the long grass.

Some time later Colette came out and leant beside me.

'It's beautiful, isn't it?' she said.

'Mm.' I wanted to go on being angry with her, but I'd been strangely calmed by the poppies and the small gardens we'd passed along the train line.

'I was just worried,' she said. 'I'm sorry.'

We stood there, the rushing air cool against our faces, as we made our way to Bologna.

Twilight

Girja Tropp

This is the summer of two-hour sleeps.

Violet roses flower and wither almost instantly. The candied petals can be added to long glasses of chilli rose drinks, a recipe given to me by my sister Ti; frozen in cubes of ice, they swish languidly as they melt and marry in the pink.

People doze ten minutes at a time for a total of two hours in a day and survive.

Smiling cracks the skin around my lips; as my husband slowly becomes ex **I become aware of the space I take up in rooms and words that have been familiar for so long take umbrage in my mouth.**

I've never pulled a trailer.

It's been booked but when I get there the service station attendant looks at me with blank eyes. On a Sunday, only one bloke serves a steady run of customers. He offers reluctant help.

The trailer follows obediently. This surprises me.

My staff sounds like she's just woken up. **Dee is a close friend.**

When I grow older and wiser, she remains young and foolish. This makes her trim and attractive to men. There is a saying about having one or the other. Big Pete is leaving with a woman twenty years younger than me. I will be fifty next July.

The faces of millions of people caught in peak hour traffic in the millions of cars are set in subtle variations of the same expression.

At last year's Twilight Market, the Mexican fiesta man was carried out on a stretcher. He will make four grand to my seven hundred dollars. I can pull out but I need mullah to pay for an expensive divorce lawyer.

Yesterday, with the neighbour's help, I put the 3 x 3 foot marquee out and blocked in where the serving person and the cooking person would stand, where the equipment would go, and how we would move around each other. Then I coloured the plan on paper so my brain would go ping at short notice. **Things to do at night between ten minute naps: Take camera into the backyard and point at sky while pressing shutter. Pull the cloud wool over and imagine a definition for safe. Create a reason for the owl that lands on the banksia bush.**

When Dee falls over the edge of a moral cliff, I get on her case. Friendship is a precious thing; it doesn't survive small knocks. That's what marriage is for, **small knocks.** She texts me back saying she will definitely help but she needs to get to the chemist and get something stronger than Panadol.

My oldest son, Dar, runs the shower out of hot water.

Dar injured his wrist in an interschool soccer match and he is to be one of my assistants at the Twilight Market but he can only do things with one hand like flipping rotis.

Drag two five kilo bags of onions, shove the esky with broken handles, stash oil tin between trestle table and gas cannister even though it is bound to fall.

Even when a thing is bound to happen, there is no time to stop it from happening. My sister Ti knew this as a young child. When learning to cycle, she would allow the accidents to come to her instead of the other way around; she would throw her hands in the air and place her palms over her eyes and allow the bike to careen unimpeded into the nearest bush.

We are an hour late, Dar reminds me.

Two minutes later, he runs back to get his wallet and locks the car keys in the house. We break a window in the laundry.

As we drive, I get Dar to ring up the names on the list of people I interviewed. Driving can be relaxing if it seems there is someplace to go. In my case, I think I am going to have a successful event despite or especially because of obstacles in my path. My sister Ti says we were lucky in the family to which we were born; since we survived, we can survive anything.

The late afternoon is no better than the morning; a big souvlaki truck is stuck in the market entrance. The road falls away sharply in front, banks off to the right. When the lights turn green, cars vroom as they cut into the traffic to their right.

A woman with henna-orange hair and prematurely wrinkled skin – I spoke to her on the telephone, the one who asked me to be brief because she had a million things to organise for the event and then sat on a brass tack and was incoherent – waves me in finally. Triple J Radio is setting up a stall on the other side of the median strip. The woman trots up and asks if we are all right. I want to know how to move the van out. She points.

Outbound traffic for stallholders starts to jam. Reversing down an entire street with stalls in the middle of set-up, and newbies mewling about being stuck, is beyond my capabilities.

The souvlaki man leaves his truck parked in a small alley (till he finds a solution) and helps.

The nineteen-year-old girl recruited from the list is making out with her boyfriend near the toilets. I pay the boyfriend to help unload. Dar gives instructions.

The girl is good with cooking. All I have to do is tell her the recipe, but her food safety is bad news; tasting by hand, forgetting to take off gloves before handling money, and scratching her head when working out sums.

During prep, I find out that I know her mother from the days I met my husband, Big Pete. She pushes strands of hair back behind pasta shell ears. 'Mum's doing an exhibition in Sydney.'

I remember. Her mother had a house with long windows and Persian carpet and was in the midst of separation. She used to sell her artwork at this market; Indian folk art nouveau, cows and animals and villages.

'She and my dad got back together last year,' the girl says. 'It was too weird having him in the house so I moved out.'

Her dad and Big Pete used to smoke bongs together. Her dad sold bongs and smoking-related paraphernalia at this market. He stopped Big Pete from killing a customer. Big Pete was one of the founding fathers of this community market.

Her mother had a body like the house she lived in, and hair like South American women in the *National Geographic*. We ought to have been kindred souls but it wasn't like that. Her eyes seemed to be far away and had an agate nature which reminded me of the time I was nine and checking in the mirror to see how beautiful I was going to be.

Dar uses both hands when he shouldn't. He keeps telling me how Big Pete would run the stall until I remind him that I'm the only bonafide Indian around and that he's only a half-breed. So he orders me home when we find the rice is missing.

Few foodies at St Andrews have power available to their stall. Normally we use a rice cooker but at St Andrews we have to bring pre-cooked rice and steam it.

On the way back, I worry about leaving Dar who is only fifteen in charge of the stall with a new girl and mistakenly take the first turnoff instead of the second, and because I can't do anything with a trailer, I can't turn around. I end up in Yarraglen and get stuck halfway into an intersection because I can't back the darn thing and there is traffic … where are they all going? And I have to take a back road towards the Lilydale airfields that takes three times as long getting home. I ring Big Pete, who is becoming my ex and who is running my second stall, and he says the Global Garden Party is sucking big time and we are going to make a loss. **When he finishes talking he says he is going to Queensland this weekend to see that woman.**

If he is going out with a woman who looks like the back end of an ass what does that say about me? I mustn't be as beautiful as I've always thought. Unlike me, she's an outdoors woman. I imagine them frothing about on a beach in wetsuits, doing it in the winter sand.

When I get back, the market looks pretty dead and Dar has given the girl permission to go and have a massage, and he's booked himself in after. They have only cooked one lot of filling for the wraps.

The girl has a disconcerting habit of taking off, unannounced, for a cigarette break and other urgencies which involve holding onto her boyfriend with both arms and talking to him in a low voice. I hear her say, 'But you can come back if you wanted.'

'No,' he says. 'Mum's got a special dinner.'

Their intensity allows me to feel older and wiser.

The organisers said ten thousand people when I was slotting in the season's events, but they didn't say the ten thousand would mainly be walking around in the shopping centre nearby. The Girl Guides Fairy Floss tent has a queue.

Dee turns up. There is a funny weeping sore on top of her forearm and she looks unwell, but she brings up the heavy sandbags needed to handle a sudden squally wind. She roll-throws these into place. Dar is looking sullen. 'You get it,' he says when I ask him for the bucket of feta.

Back from the loo, I find Dee in a fit. Apparently some child insisted on curry and then didn't want it and the mother came back saying that we ought to have our licences taken away for selling curry so hot.

I pour the chilli rose drinks into long tumblers. (Big Pete warned me about lugging glassware around in trailers; said it was a hassle and nearly dissuaded me.) The ice cubes spin around and the petals flirt with the edges till they finally rise to the top. I put row upon row out the front on a trestle table. This makes for a convoluted journey to the bain-marie and cash register but somehow people stop; they pick up the glasses and admire the colour and they ask me about the petals, at which point I direct their attention to the bain-marie and tell them what they would like to eat. **People are relieved to be told what they would like to eat. They don't want to boldly announce their ignorance but are happy, even though wary of spruiking, to be schmoozed towards some new exotic taste.**

There is a lot of love in the food you make, Ti says, but sometimes there is no time left. **All the things we do for love are the same as the things we do for duty.** I have to help Ti out of trouble this week; she rescued a Doberman pup from a twenty-eight-year-old Italian with a BMW convertible. He was going to dump it in an empty lot, changed his mind and then changed it again. Now he wants the pup back. But Ti looked after it for a month and then found a home with a childless couple. He was good-looking, says Ti, but a hoon with no brains, and I only flirted a little so I could save the pup. Ti, who is fifty next July, is petrified that her husband will find out or that she will be bashed up by the said hoon.

There is a rich blue patch in my sky that bleeds into the overtaking grey. I never saw it till Big Pete left. Ti remembers our father being a kind and caring man who gave her presents. Her memories are borrowed from her favourite movies.

The girl says her boyfriend will help with pack-up, and he comes, then he does the same disappearing trick she is prone to, and joins a group of long-haired almost-men with rollies hanging out the corners of their mouths and guitars slung casually over hunched shoulders.

I rearrange the gas tanks flush against the cookers with Petra's help. She screams. I look up. Big hairy things are dropping from the trees. **Fear of spiders can be cured by fatigue.** Tomorrow I have another event, a new one, in a suburb that's difficult to navigate.

The wrinkled woman begs us to come back for the Heidelberg festival, promising that it will be much better and more suited to our ambience. 'What does ambience mean?' Dar asks on the way home.

'It means, thank you very much for all your help.'

'I don't feel well,' he says in a sulky voice.

'Nor do I.'

The house is quiet. Dar has gone out and is staying out. My bones have dissolved on the sofa and my eyes are settling into the dwindling light and changing patterns in the garden. Before we arrived home, I stopped to get the makings of a cocktail. There is a slice of leftover choc fudge on a saucer. I am high on my tiredness, my mind has vanished into a sea of muscle pain, brain torpor and cellular karate.

A patch of blue blooms in my sky. This is something I am unlikely to be able to share. My hallucinations allow me to see more vividly when I am miserable or when I am making someone else's life miserable. **I am one of the faces of millions of people interpreting the sky as they careen in and out of control of their lives.**

Cloud Busting

Tara June Winch

We go cloud busting, Billy and me, down at the beach, belly up to the big sky. We make rainbows that pour out from the tops of our heads, squinting our eyes into the gathering. Fairy-flossed pincushion clouds explode. We hold each other's hand; squeeze really hard to build up the biggest brightest rainbow and bang! Shoot it up to the sky, bursting cloud suds that scatter escaping into the air alive.

We toss our bodies off the eelgrass-covered dunes and down to the shore where seaweed beads trace the waterline. Little bronze teardrops – we bust them too. Bubble-wrapped pennies.

We collect pipis, squirming our heels into the shallow water, digging deeper under the sandy foam. Reaching down for our prize, we find lantern shells, cockles, and sometimes periwinkles, bleached white. We snatch them up filling our pockets. We find shark egg capsules like dried-out leather corkscrews and cuttlebones and sand snail skeletons, and branches, petrified to stone. We find coral clumps, sponge tentacles and sea mats, and bluebottles – we bust with a stick. We find weed ringlet dolls' wigs and strings of brown pearls; I wear them as bracelets. We get drunk on the salt air and laughter. We dance, wiggling our bottoms from the dunes' heights. We crash into the surf, we swim, we dive, and we tumble. We empty our lungs and weight ourselves cross-legged to the seabed; there we have tea parties underwater. Quickly, before we swim up for mouthfuls of air.

We're not scared of the ocean, that doesn't come until later. When we're kids we have no fear, it gets sucked out in the rips. We swim with the current, like breeding turtles and hidden stingrays as we slither out onto the sand.

We climb the dunes again, covered in sticky sand and sea gifts. We ride home and string up dry sea urchins at our window. We break open our pipis and our mum places each half under the grill or fries them in the saucepan, with onion and tomatoes. We empty our pockets and line the seashells along the windowsill. My mum starts on about the saucepans; she wants to tell us stories even though we know most of them off by heart, over and over, every detail. The saucepans she says, the best bloody saucepans.

Billy and me sit at the window while she fries and begins her story. I'm still busting clouds through the kitchen pane, as they pass over the roof guttering and explode quietly in my rainbow.

It was Goulburn, 1967, Mum would begin. Where's that? We'd say. Somewhere far away, a Goulburn that doesn't exist anymore, she'd answer, and carry on with her story.

Anyway, Goulburn, '67. All my brothers and sisters had been put into missions by then, except Fred who went to live with my mother's sister. And me, I was with my mother, probably cos my skin's real dark, see, but that's another story, you don't need to know that. So old Mum and me, we're sent to Goulburn from the river, to live in these little flats, tiny things. Flatettes or something. Mum was working for a real nice family, at the house cooking and cleaning; they were so nice to old Mum.

I would go to work with her, used to sit outside and play and wait for her to finish. And when we came home Mum would throw her feet up on the balcony rail, roll off her stockings and smoke her cigarettes in the sun. Maybe talk with the other women, most of them were messed about, climbing those walls, trying to forget. It wasn't a good time for the women, losing their children.

Anyway, all us women folk were sitting up there this hot afternoon and down on the path arrived this white man, all suited up. Mum called down to him, I don't know why, she didn't know him. I remember she said, 'Hey there mister, what you got there?' A box was tucked under his arm. He looked up at all of us and smiled. He come dashing up the stairwell and onto our balcony. I think he would've been the only white person to ever step up there. He was smooth.

'Good afternoon to you ladies. In this box, I am carrying the best saucepans in the land.'

Mum sucked on her cigarette and stubbed it out in the tin. 'Give us a look then.'

The suit opened up the box and arranged the saucepans on the balcony, the stainless steel shining and twinkling in the sun. They were magical. All the women whooped and wooed at the saucepans. They really were perfect. Five different sizes and a Dutch oven, for cakes. Strong black grooved handles on the sides and the lids, the real deal.

'How much?' Mum said, getting straight to the point. The suit started up then on his big speech about the saucepans: Rena ware, 18/10, only the best, and this and that, lifetime guarantee, all that sort of stuff. The women started laughing. They knew what the punchline was going to be, nothing that they could afford, ever. Their laughter cascaded over the balcony's rails as they followed each other back into the shade of their rooms. 'Steady there Alice, you got a little one to feed there too!' they said, seeing Mum still entranced as they went inside.

Mum sat there, watching his mouth move and the sun bouncing off the pans. He told her the price, something ridiculous, and Mum didn't even flinch. She lit up another fag, puffed away. I think he was surprised, maybe relieved that she didn't throw him out, and he rounded off his speech. Mum just sat there as he packed up the saucepans, getting himself together to leave. 'You not gunna let me buy 'em then?' Mum said, blowing smoke above our heads.

'Would you like to, Miss?'

'Of course I bloody do, wouldna sat here waiting for you to finish if I didn't!'

He laughed. Mum told him then that she couldn't afford it, but she wanted them. So they made a deal. Samuel, the travelling salesman, would come by once a month, when money would come from the family, and he would take a payment each time.

Mum worked extra hours from then on, sometimes taking home the ironing, hoping to get a little more from the lady of the house. And she did, just enough. And Samuel would come round and chat with Mum and the ladies and bring sweets for me. He and Mum would be chatting and drinking tea until it got dark outside. They became friends after all that time. Three years and seven months it took her. When Samuel came round on his last visit, with a box under his arm, just like the first time, Mum smiled big. He came into the flat and placed the box on the kitchen bench. 'Open it,' he said to Mum, and smiled down at me and winked.

Mum pressed down the sides of her uniform then folded open the flaps and lifted out each saucepan, weighing them in her hands and squinting over at Samuel, puzzled. With each lid she pulled off tears gathered and fell. 'What is it, what is it?' I was saying, as I pulled a chair up against the bench. Under one lid was a big leg of meat, under another potatoes and carrots, a shiny chopping knife, then a bunch of eggs, then bread. And in the Dutch oven, a wonky-looking steamed pudding. Mum was crying too much to laugh at the cake.

'I haven't got a hand for baking yet. Hope you don't mind I tested it out?' Mum just shook her head, she couldn't say a word and I think Samuel understood. He put on his smart hat, tilting it at Mum, and said, 'Good day to you, Alice, good day, young lady.'

And when Mum passed, she gave the pots to me.

When my mother finished her stories she'd be crying too, tiny streams down her cheekbones. I knew she would hock everything we ever owned, except the only things we did – five size-ranged saucepans, with Dutch oven. Still their hard metal case, only a few handles chipped. I run my fingertips over fingerprints now, over years, generations. They haven't changed much, they still linger patiently. They still smell of friendship. I suppose that to my grandmother, Samuel was much like a cloud buster. Letting in some hope from the sun. Their rainbow had been their friendship. And I suppose that to my mum, Samuel was someone who she wanted to stay around, like a blue sky. To Samuel, my mum and grandmother, I don't know, maybe the exchange was even, and maybe when those clouds burst open, he got to feel the rain. A cleaning rain and maybe, that was enough.

Honeymoon

Charlotte Wood

The night they arrive at the house on the lake, Mandy slides open the door to the deck and a tiny grey possum clambers down a tree trunk, an arm's length from the railing.

'Matt, look,' she calls. She takes a step onto the deck. Another possum, bigger than the first, darts down the tree behind it and the two animals leap on to the wooden railing. Mandy stops. The possums fix their gaze on her, lowering their small heads, eyes shining. She steps forward again – and then both the animals thump gracelessly onto the wooden boards and pelt towards her feet.

'Jesus!' she yelps, jumping back behind the screen door and slinging it shut.

The possums stop still for one long second, watching her again. Then they waddle about on the deck, sniffing.

Matthew appears behind her, 'Oh, wow.' He reaches for the door.

'Don't go out there!' She grabs his arm. Then feels her face colour. 'They ran at me. Somebody must feed them.'

Matthew stands on the hairy orange carpet next to her, his new wife. He takes her hand from his arm, smiles down at her.

'Mand, it's just a mum and her baby.' Then he puts an arm around her shoulders. 'I'll get them some fruit,' he says. But he begins stroking Mandy's arm in long, firm strokes. 'It's OK,' he says, his voice soothing.

She shrugs her shoulder away. 'I'm all right.'

When Mandy came home from uni to her parents' small town and told them she was getting married, her dad said, 'Christ.'

Matthew was coming the next day. He said she should wait for him before making the announcement, that it was selfish not to. She couldn't say she wanted to protect him.

Her mother said, 'Heavens.' Then, 'That's wonderful, isn't it Geoff!'

Her dad said, 'You're only twenty-one. There's plenty of time.'

Mandy had put down her glass of champagne – she'd brought the bottle herself, opened it while they watched on, nervous, expectant. She looked at her fingertips turning white from pressing the base of the glass, and said, 'How old were you, Dad?'

Her mother twittered. 'Wonderful!' she said, and sipped the drink, glassy-eyed already. But Mandy and her father locked gazes.

He said, 'It doesn't matter, because I wasn't doing anything important.'

Mandy threw her head back. 'Jesus! That's great.' She turned to her mother, who was blinking quickly, the way she did when she met someone new, or spoke to someone she thought important in some way – tilting her head back a little, smiling, but flitting her lashes so fast they were almost completely shut.

'Sorry, Mum.'

Her mum gave her head a little shake, still blinking and sipping.

Her dad growled, 'You know what I mean.'

He meant university. Honours, maybe even a medal. Mandy stretched her arms above her head, and closed her eyes tight for a second to force away the tears she could feel beginning.

'I'm not an idiot, Dad.'

Then she lifted her glass, said, 'Well, here's to us. Thanks for your enthusiasm. You can congratulate Matt when he gets here tomorrow.'

She drank and stood up. Her dad watched her, the glass stem dainty between his big fingers. 'I'm thinking about your future,' he said. Then he muttered, 'I don't want you to limit yourself.' He glanced towards his wife, and then quickly away again.

But Mandy was already striding across the room, leaning down to her mother.

'Thanks Mum,' she whispered, and kissed her soft face while her mother began shuffling her body out of the chair.

In the kitchen Cathy was coming through the back door, breathless, in her school uniform, smelling of cigarettes. 'Hi,' the sisters both said, as Cathy slung her backpack to the floor. Mandy said, 'I'm going out,' and slammed the door.

At the lake house there is a garage with old surfboards and plastic skis, and a tinny with a heavy, sluggish outboard motor. On the first afternoon they take the boat out. Matthew knows how to work the motor and sits next to it, hugging it one-armed while they putter across the water. 'Let's do this every day,' he shouts as the green water slides beneath them.

But Mandy has seen the kayak. In the morning she eases herself out of bed without waking Matthew, and goes barefoot to the kitchen to make coffee. She frowns at the noise of the electric kettle as it boils.

She picks her way down through the prickly bush garden to the water and hoists the white and yellow kayak off the grass, holding it across her hips, tilting herself backwards to balance the weight. She steps over the stones, and then lowers it – *plop* – into the water. With her fingertips she directs it between some rocks so it won't float away in the mild slapping of the water. Then she wades ankle-deep to the furthest rock and sets down her coffee cup on its flattest part. She wades back and lowers herself into the kayak seat, making the boat rock wonkily. She shunts her bum forward and uses the white plastic oar to push off from the stones, feeling the kayak grazing the underwater pebbles. She reaches for the cup and then, holding it aloft in one hand, digs a few one-handed strokes with the other, out into the deeper water. Then she lays the bar of the paddle across her lap and sips from the cup, letting the kayak drift out into the vast grey sheet of the lake. Almost as far as she can see ahead and to each side, is the metallic water.

She sits back, closing her eyes against the sunlight, knees bent. The water shrugs beneath her. Then she drains the cup and sets it on the floor, and paddles a few neat strokes with the sun at her back. She drifts over to where she has seen some fish jumping and sits very still, listening for the tiny splash, scanning for the movement. Then there it is, the *plish*, the glimpse of small white fish arched in the air above the silver water.

Every morning she does this, paddling and drifting for an hour on the silent lake, before Matthew wakes.

The wedding had been the usual thing for her home town. Ceremony in the park by the river (not Saint Mark's, after several arguments with her mother). The celebrant was a woman in a cream nylon suit and an aqua blouse, they'd read something from Kahlil Gibran. Afterwards, at the reception in the Corroboree Room behind the civic hall, Mandy sat at the round bridal table with Matthew, her parents, and her sister Cathy.

The smell of the wood panelling in the Corroboree Room reminded her of their afternoons there as children when their father had supplied the sound system for football club functions. In his youth, he had wanted to be a sound engineer. So he owned a mixing board and many long extension cords, he owned big stippled silver cases with snap locks, amps and various players, folding stands, large black speakers in scratched black chipboard casings and three microphones with stands of varying heights. He didn't need these things for his job at the gas company, but he liked to have them. While he spent

Saturday afternoons of their childhood laying out cables and saying 'check, check' into the microphones, Mandy and Cathy had the Corroboree Room to themselves, sliding on the polished green lino and sitting in the crook of the one wooden step up to the stage.

At the wedding Mandy wore a dress made by her university friends and her mother sat next to Matthew. Her mum had secretly liked Matthew from the start. He played up to her, teased her in a way that made Mandy wonder if her father had ever done this, because her mother flushed and looked younger whenever she and Matthew bantered. Mandy imagined her dad – young, slim, broad-shouldered – teasing her mother about her hips, or her tea towels, the way Matthew did.

The second night at the lake they set the outdoor table on the deck for dinner, sticking candles into wine bottles, the candlelight making the trees flicker. Matthew has made a big bowl of spaghetti and stands over Mandy like a waiter, using tongs to lift the pasta on to her plate. Then there's a noise, and they look up to see the big possum angling its way down the tree again, one side of its body moving forward then the other, its snout lifting in purposeful, rhythmic nods.

'Shit,' Mandy says.

'It's OK, it won't come near us,' says Matthew.

But the possum leaps on to the railing and stalks towards them. The smaller one has appeared now too, waddling behind its mother.

Mandy stands, scraping her chair loudly and shoving it in the animals' direction. 'Shoo!'

The candle flames wobble. The possums stop. They stare at her, their dingy feather-duster tails held up in the air.

Mandy drags the chair again, looks around for Matthew, who has disappeared. She feels stupid. The dinner is getting cold. But the mother possum begins to walk again, delicately, along the railing, stretching her face towards the table. Mandy steps back, thinks of the possum's mean little teeth, the tiny fleas and bacteria in its fur.

Matt appears with a long, spindly piece of eucalypt branch. He steps forward and whacks the stick down, hard, on the decking. The possums straighten, staring. He cracks the stick down again, harder, and the noise echoes up into the dark around the house. The possums turn and amble along the railing towards the bedroom at the end of the house, into the darkness.

Mandy pulls her chair back towards the table. 'Thanks,' she mumbles, glancing past Matthew into the gloom. She can't see them.

Matt grins and says, 'I'll put some music on.'

On the nights after this they each sit with a thin branch leaned against their chair. Every night the possums come, then retreat into the shadows at the cracking of the sticks.

Sometimes Mandy looks up from the table to see their eyes shining out of the dark.

Matthew was a city boy when they met at a party in her first weeks at university. 'Never been west of the Blue Mountains,' he'd said airily, lighting a cigarette.

He wore a black suit jacket with his black jeans, listened to The Cruel Sea. When she said she didn't know who The Cruel Sea were he was incredulous. 'Tex Perkins. The *Cruel Sea.*'

She was blank. 'Sorry.'

He took the cigarette from his mouth and blew a long stream of smoke. 'You really *are* a country girl,' he said, and then he smiled, a wide, city-boy smile. Later they had sex in his room in the dark, the party babbling outside his bedroom door, beneath the mournful music coming from his battered CD player.

'I like your body,' he whispered, propped on his elbow in the gloom. He said *breasts,* as though it were not a foreign word for a boy. He drew a sharp line down her breastbone with his fingernail. She liked his spiky confidence. He switched on a lamp with a sarong covering it – he had been to Asia – and low orange light washed the room. He sat up in bed and began rolling a joint.

She lay naked on top of the sheets, feeling on her skin an echo of the line he had traced down her sternum. A corner of her future was opening up.

Long before the wedding, the first time she brought Matthew home, her mother made up Cathy's room for him, with the good sheets, the new pillowcases. Mandy had snuck into the room after they'd all gone to bed, squeezed in beside him, snickering at his clump of black clothes and his motorbike boots heaped on the floor next to Cathy's pale pink chest of drawers. She touched his nipple.

'Don't,' he whispered. 'Your parents.'

She laughed again, bent to lick it.

'It's not fair on them,' he murmured, gently pushing her away. 'They're nice people.'

She stared at him in the dark, and then she stood up and padded back through the silent house to lie in her childhood bed, listening to her sister asleep, breathing slow and heavy on a mattress on the floor.

At the lake they spend the days sitting on the deck, looking out at the water through the trees, newspapers strewn about them, listening to seed pods dropping onto the corrugated iron roof. The house is full of ugly, comfortable furniture they sink into. Prehistoric-looking couches with the nap worn off the fake suede, with seat cushions so deep their feet don't touch the floor. There is a smoked-glass coffee table with battered board games on a shelf beneath. Scattegories and Monopoly and obscure, failed board games: Payday, and How to Be a Complete Bastard with Adrian Edmonson's face all over the box.

The maroon milk crate filled with their uni textbooks and foolscap notebooks stays by the front door, untouched.

Sometimes they have sex, quietly, on the clean white sheets with the sun falling into the room, only the screen door between them and the cicadas and the chittering of the lorikeets.

The next time he had gone home with her was for Easter.

'Do you want to go with them?' Matthew had asked her at breakfast, while her mother scurried around the house before Mass, checking her handbag, putting on lipstick at the hallway mirror.

Mandy had only snorted, and poured another coffee. 'Have you got any cigarettes?' she asked him.

'Shhh,' he whispered, angling his head towards her mother, who was now in the kitchen prodding at a solid white-plasticked chicken defrosting on the sink.

Cathy grinned at Matthew over her Weetbix. 'Wuss,' she said with her mouth full, spoon aloft.

'Come on Cathy,' called their mother. 'And you shouldn't be eating breakfast so late.' Their parents never ate before Communion.

They went to buy Easter eggs and hot cross buns after collecting her parents from Mass. At the supermarket checkout they watched the coloured eggs and the plastic bags of buns moving along the conveyor belt.

Cathy said, 'There's Sue McInerney.'

At the next counter a thin girl from Cathy's year stood with a lanky, slightly older boy, lifting things from a trolley; frozen food boxes and bags of corn chips and sheets of pale sausages.

'I remember her,' Mandy said. 'Brainy.'

Cathy flicked a red egg, sending it spinning in circles on the conveyor belt. 'Pregnant, apparently.'

The sisters raised their eyebrows at each other.

Matthew took out his wallet, but Mandy's father was standing ahead of them, a fifty dollar note ready in his hand. He was watching Sue McInerney too, until Cathy nudged his elbow for the waiting checkout girl.

As they were driving home Matthew looked out of the window at the yellowing trees. He said, 'It's quite beautiful here really. I could live here.' He didn't look at Mandy, but was watching the back of her father's head. 'When we finish uni,' he added.

Dad looked only at the road.

After lunch that day the family drifted into silence. Dad was slouched in his armchair, reading a Thomas Keneally book with his glasses halfway down his nose. Cathy was at the end of the couch, with a little collection of nail polish remover and enamels and cuticle-softener bottles arranged before her on the coffee table. She had a foot up on the table, rubbing a nail with a cotton ball. Their mother had put on Handel's *Messiah*, as she did at every family occasion. Mandy lay on the carpet reading a magazine, propped up on her elbow. In quiet parts of the music she could hear her mother and Matthew chatting in the kitchen over the washing up. He was saying something about the local council and town planning jobs.

One morning out in the kayak she sees one of the enormous pale jellyfish they'd noticed much further out in the deeper water, from the boat. Now it glides alongside her. She wants to touch its fleshy, globular tentacles, the huge thickened dome of its head. She strokes the water once with the paddle to keep up, following its slow-motion dipping and surfacing. But after a while the jellyfish sinks deeper, and though she stares hard into the dark water as it lowers, it disappears.

The sun is hotter now. She turns to see the house in the distance, the shape of Matthew hunched over the railing of the deck, looking out across the lake towards her.

She waves, then dips the paddle straight down, feels the boat rotate, graceful as a dancer.

At the wedding her father talked into one of his microphones, huskily welcoming Matthew into the family, but looking at Mandy. She smiled back at him. Later, father and daughter danced awkwardly together. She was a little drunk. She called, through a space in the song, into her father's ear, 'You've been happy, haven't you Dad?' He grunted, 'Oh, love. Course I have.' Then he said, 'I'm sorry about before.' And she put her head into his shoulder to stop herself from crying.

Over the week she teaches herself how to control the kayak, experimenting by keeping her elbows at her sides or lifting them, or by shifting her grip along the paddle. Sometimes she moves through the water smooth and fast, as though propelled by some force beyond herself. At other times she can't wield the paddle; it smacks at the water or bangs down on the side of the boat, causing it to wobble and rock. But on each outing she spends much of the time simply drifting, gazing into the water. Sometimes she comes across a single patch of bubbles. She tries to stare into the depths, but once again there's nothing to be seen except the sliding, bulbous surface of the water itself.

One morning she sees the small red swatch of a kite high in the air.

When she and Cathy were small their father had had a brief kite-flying craze, driving his reluctant girls to the highest of the bare hills near the town. He would lift his kites, delicate creations of dowel and bright tissue paper, from the boot of the car. Mandy would huddle in her nylon parka, hair whipping her face in the freezing wind. 'I told you to wear something warmer,' her father growled while he untangled a cord. But Mandy had insisted on her pink tartan skirt and bare legs, and the wind was icy. The girls had to stand, each holding a skein of nylon line in both hands, while their father strode up the hill ahead of them. Then he would throw up each of the kites and shout, 'Run!', and they had to run over the knobbly tussocky ground, holding the lines high above their heads. The kite would mostly swirl once or twice and arrow straight towards the stony ground. But sometimes, sometimes, it would lift, and the spool would whirl and tumble in her hands, the purple kite lifting higher and higher, and Mandy would begin to smile, and Cathy's green box kite would lift and she would shriek, her head thrown back and mouth wide open, and their father would stand and watch his children falling in love with the high space beyond that small town, with the possibilities of flight.

Now Mandy looks up at the distant red kite in the blue sky

above the lake, anchored to somewhere on the distant shore. She remembers the rhythmic tug on the line, calibrating its pull against the weight of her own body, the pleasure of letting out the line, then resisting. She turns from it then, and paddles towards the centre of the lake. But all morning, it seems the kite stays with her, always above her, there in the outer corner of her sight.

The wind rises. She churns back through the water towards the house, breathing deep and rhythmically, pushing the high end of the paddle forward with all the strength of one arm as she dips deep and pulls the low end through the water with the other hand, the choppy little waves slapping over the prow of the kayak.

Afterwards she walks up the garden, her arms and legs pleasantly jittery from the last long stretch of effort.

When she slides open the glass door Matthew is reading the paper at the table.

'I said I was going to come with you,' he says crossly. 'But you didn't wake me up.'

The room feels small and airless after the wide gusty space of the lake, the red star of the kite stamped in the sky.

'Oh, sorry,' she says, as she passes his chair. 'I forgot.'

At noon they gather provisions to go out in the boat for the afternoon. Matthew waits on the deck, hands full with a fishing rod and one plastic shopping bag of bait, and another holding lunch things – a half-bottle of wine with a cork jammed into it, some bread and cheese. His straw hat dangles, sunglasses glint on his head.

Mandy puts a hand to the bench for the door keys, but they aren't there. Matthew watches her from outside, shifting his weight while she scrabbles through the things on the bench: coins, unopened envelopes, a banana, a bottle of sunscreen, three pens, some national park brochures.

'Hang on,' she calls, moving to the other end of the bench where the owners keep a basket full of miscellaneous stuff. She peers into it. Fishing lures, magnets, pens, more sunscreen, a computer disk, some cassettes with the brown tape knotted in loops, a plastic tub of moisturiser.

'Come on,' calls Matthew, irritated.

She straightens. 'I can't find the keys.' She walks to the door. 'Did you have them or did I?'

Matthew groans. 'You did, because when we got home you opened the door and I carried in the shopping.'

This is true. She turns back, hands on her hips, thinking, scanning the room. The keys have an enormous plastic Bananas in Pyjamas key ring. Impossible to lose. Suddenly she feels a wave of dislike for Matthew, standing there ready for a picnic.

'Are you going to help me look?' she asks, hands still on her hips.

He sighs, puts down the fishing rod and the bags, jostling them into a corner of shade by the door. She thinks she sees his eyebrows lift as he bends, pushing the things about noisily, but when he stands again he is smiling tightly. She wants, suddenly, to smack him on his smooth, shaven face.

'I don't know where the fucking things are,' she says viciously, and begins striding about the room, flipping cushions and snapping pieces of paper.

'Don't worry, we'll find them,' he says. But making it clear, in his tone, that the delay is her fault.

They each begin to wander round the house, bending and straightening as they search, and he calls out questions. 'Did you take them out of the front door?'

'*Yes.*' She hurries to check. Not there.

'What did you do then?'

From the hallway she can see him now in the bedroom, lifting shorts and shirts to shoulder height, listening for keys in pockets.

'I don't *know.*'

He keeps yelling out questions, which she doesn't answer.

She moves, her body bent, through the rooms, lifting every cushion again, running a hand beneath each one. When she comes back to the kitchen he's standing in front of the rubbish bin below the bench. 'I guess we should empty it. They could have fallen in.'

She does not think the keys could have fallen in. They would need to fall at a 45-degree angle, backwards and under the lip of the bench top. But she has nothing better to offer. 'Mmmm,' she says.

She can feel her temperature rising, a headache beginning. They have been looking for twenty minutes. Matthew is still standing at the bin, hands on hips, his back to her. She is beginning to feel a panicky pain beneath her ribs. But Matthew is quite calm, standing there watching the bin as though it were a view.

It *is* her fault. This fact makes her angrier.

'Where the – ' she lifts a pile of heavy books and then lets them fall from a height, slamming on to the table '– *fuck* are they!'

She falls into one of the chairs, grabbing shoes from the floor, shaking each one.

She looks across at Matthew. 'What if we don't find them?'

She hears her voice, the sound of her own panic. He doesn't turn around, doesn't answer.

'What are we going to *do, Matt?*'

Then as she watches him she sees his hands in his pockets. He turns around slowly. She stares at him, and he smiles.

He's got them.

'It's OK babe, calm down, we'll find them.' He takes his hands – carefully, it seems now – out of his pockets, steps towards her across the orange carpet that reminds her, suddenly, of pubic hair. He leans down and puts two hands on her shoulders. She feels her body stiffen, her head is hot.

'Are you sure you didn't put them in your pocket accidentally?' she asks slowly, keeping her voice even, looking him in the eyes. He rears back, making a face. 'Course I'm sure!' But his hands stay on her bare brown shoulders. She glances down at his pockets, trying to see any possible shape, but he moves off, soundless, back into the kitchen, and bends to open the fridge door. 'My flatmate once put keys in the fridge,' he says, squinting into the square of light, reaching in to shift jars and bottles.

Mandy goes to the bathroom. She feels sick. She remembers the possums, his stroking her arm.

Breathe. It's ridiculous; of course he doesn't have them.

They have just gotten married.

She hears the fridge door close and then another noise, his voice. She runs into the kitchen.

'Ah, shit. Sorry, nope. My car keys.' He holds them up.

But he's still smiling that odd little smile. She sees him glance back at the rubbish bin.

Mandy's heart begins to jolt in her chest. She walks to the bin.

'I'll do that,' Matthew says, but he stays where he is, running a hand lightly along the top of the fridge.

She feels all the blood has gone out of her somehow, she is suddenly exhausted. 'It's OK,' she murmurs. 'I lost them, I'll do it.'

He says, 'Babe, don't be like that.' But he doesn't move.

She hauls the heavy, thin plastic bag out of the bin, across the carpet and over the sharp lip of the metal frame of the sliding door. The bag tears and liquid oozes out. She grabs newspaper from the outdoor table and crawls around the deck, spreading the pages about. She does not care that Matthew is standing there, watching her.

On the hot boards of the deck she crouches, upends the sweating black plastic and the thick, foetid smell springs up at her as the chicken bones and rotten fruit and oyster shells and nameless bits of sludge slide out. She lifts the bag away and a last wad of prawn shells falls wetly on her bare foot. The pink shells, and now her foot, are covered with tiny crawling ants.

She kneels then, in the rubbish, not bothering to flick off the ants, picking through the sodden remnants of the garbage with her fingers, knowing she will not find the glint of metal there in the coffee grounds and onion skins and band-aids, among the screwed-up tissues and the black plastic trays dripping with red meat juice.

She thinks of her father's warm, rough hands over her own seven-year-old ones, holding the whirring kite spool. She thinks of all his disappointments.

She does not look up when she hears Matthew cry out triumphantly from the living room. He appears in the doorway, holding up the keys on their huge blue and yellow plastic glob. 'Would you believe it, under the bloody magazines! I'll just have a piss and then we can go.'

And smiling his smile, he tosses her the keys where she kneels.

She catches them in her two hands, cupped against her chest. She feels the sharp edges hit her breastbone.

The True Daughter

Danielle Wood

1.

'Kate,' says Faye, 'is a mezzo soprano. For which I am grateful, actually.'

There is opera playing, and it seems, to Tamsin, to occupy Faye's apartment as if it were part of the décor; the rich voice echoing off the timber of the furniture, rippling over near-white carpet as soft as the fleece of a newborn lamb.

'I suspect sopranos are flightier, altogether more given to tantrums and putting on airs and graces. I don't see how it can possibly be good for your equilibrium, spending all that time in the upper registers. Also, sopranos are invariably blonde.'

Tamsin smiles. It is the morning of her first day and already she thinks that she will like Faye. She does not, however, think that she will like Kate. Tamsin suspects her to be the sort of daughter who will leave it until the very end. Then she will jet in, all European couture and big sunglasses, just in time to perform a day or two of lower-register histrionics and take the starring role at the funeral. Most likely, she will be the type to treat her mother's nurses like so many hired hands, despatching them to the kitchen for more tea, or to the bathroom for more tissues. Kate, Tamsin can already tell, will be the sort of woman to make her feel, keenly, the girlishness of her plain brown ponytail.

*

It hardly matters, since it is more or less everywhere now, where it began. But when Tamsin undresses Faye for her sponge bath, the origin is clear. Beneath the bodice of her nightgown Faye's chest, without its breasts, is as profoundly nude as an unfeathered baby bird. Tamsin sponges over the buckled scarring, gently, apologising to the skin for the indignities it has already suffered.

'They were rather nice, you know. I didn't know that, of course, when I had them,' Faye says as Tamsin buttons up the front of a clean gown. 'Still, at least I passed their likeness on to Kate.'

Tamsin draws up a vial of morphia and stretches out the bone and fine hide of Faye's arm. A brisk slap to the arm's crook and the needle slips unnoticed into the still-stinging skin.

'That barely hurt at all,' Faye says, and Tamsin cannot prevent the corners of her mouth from turning up, just a little.

'There is a bit of an art to it,' she admits.

In the afternoon Faye sleeps, opera turned down low. Her bed is in the front room now, along with all of her paintings. The rest of the apartment has a ransacked look, picture-hooks hanging bare on cream walls marked by faint rectangles of absence. Cluttered together on two large windowless walls, the paintings make a jigsaw puzzle gallery, just inches between their frames. When Tamsin looks closely, she finds that she knows them already. Almost. She knows their shapes and colours, but not their precise configurations. She looks until she understands that they are painters' other works; the equivalent, perhaps, of photographs taken a few moments before or after the perfect shot. Tamsin stands for a long time before a melon-breasted, tangle-limbed nude who reclines by a window filled with the ultramarine of Sydney Harbour, and decides that Faye has taste, as well as money.

She thinks that she will like this job. As always, she doesn't know how long it will last, but it is better paid than most. If she is disciplined about setting some of her wages aside, perhaps it will not be so much of a struggle next time to make it through the weeks or months before someone else begins in earnest to die, and can afford the luxury of doing it in their own home. She had tried not to look pleasantly surprised when Faye's nephew, who had interviewed her for the job, named his price. Impressed by her references, he brought her into this room to meet Faye, and she remembers now how all the while that they talked his eyes caressed the walls.

At the end of the day Tamsin leaves Faye in the care of the night nurse and rides home on her bike. There is a quicker way but Tamsin does not take it. Even here, out on the far edge of the arcing route she follows, she can feel the pull of the place she is avoiding. It has become a gaping hole in the outskirts of her city, a swirling plughole of orange bricks, which threatens to suck in first the neighbouring buildings, then the architecture of the surrounding blocks, then the suburbs in concentric rings until the spiralling devastation reaches out as far as the small weatherboard house where Tamsin lives, not happily anymore, with Michael.

2.

'Kate,' says Faye, 'has true auburn hair. The sort of hair I would rather have liked for myself, I confess.'

Tamsin can imagine this true auburn hair – long, loosely curling, sweeping back from Kate's dramatic face. She pictures Kate with the square, capacious jaw of a diva and a chin perpetually upthrust. In her publicity photos she would wear deep green velvet, a portrait neckline gesturing down to the healthy flesh of her breasts.

'She was a wonderful Cenerentola, when she was younger. She does Rosina well, too, but it's Orfeo that she's known for.'

'Orfeo?'

'As in Orpheus. Pants role. The soprano plays Euridice.'

'Tragic ending, I assume.'

'Actually Gluck has Amor, the god of love, take pity on Orfeo and bring Euridice back to life in the final act.'

'That was generous of him.'

'I suspect he felt it was only fair to finish with a big chorus and some swooning,' she says. And then she giggles. 'I must bear that in mind myself.'

Faye's giggle is one of the things Tamsin likes most about her. It is a delighted, girlish giggle, and far from being at odds with her old-woman's face, it gives purpose to every crease. When Faye giggles, Tamsin does too. She has never known anyone to approach death so cheerfully, as if it were just a thing she had never got round to doing before.

By the end of her first week with Faye, Tamsin is riding home by a still-longer route, widening her circle of avoidance. It leads her through a suburb she has never before had reason to visit, down a short street with cafés and shops full of inessential and expensive things. Women she suspects are doctors' wives return to glossy cars with armloads of flowers.

She stands by the window of a small boutique, guilty and furtive. She looks in and sees, browsing through racks of tiny clothes, women whose peculiarly shaped bodies show that they have nothing to hide. Tamsin thinks of the babies inside them, plump as broad beans, securely attached to their vines. If these women looked at her, Tamsin wonders, would they know? Could they tell? Is there a mark? Does it show? She waits until the shop is empty of customers before she enters. She buys a hat, in the very smallest size. It is white. She does not know enough to choose something pink or blue.

Wits about her, Tamsin rides through fumy, traffic-thick streets. She thinks of her house, which will already be occupied by Michael; his university books open on the kitchen table, his cooking in the pot. She takes a detour and cycles twice around a lake whose still surface reflects the darkening sky.

3.

'Kate,' says Faye, 'married well. She took my advice on that matter. I told her to look not for an adversary, but for a rock.'

Tamsin supposes that when Kate does appear, it will be with this husband-of-Gibraltar in obedient tow. She makes a mental note to check whether or not his jumper is the same colour as his wife's ensemble of suitcases.

'And I told her that it would be best if he were tone deaf, too. That way he could only ever admire her, and never be tempted to criticise.'

Tamsin doesn't know whether Faye's advice to her daughter on the subject of husbands was the result of Faye's having herself married an adversary or a rock, someone who was tone deaf or someone who had a tendency to criticise. She would like to know, but it is not her way to ask questions of her patients. In part this is because she is a nurse whose task it is to bring ease, not to prod at what might turn out to be invisible bruises. But it is also because she finds it less interesting to engage in the anxious, hasty excavation of inquiry than to wait and see which fragments of a life – here at life's end – are the ones her patients consider important enough to share.

At the end of her first month, Tamsin knows only that Faye's husband was a surgeon. Called Keith. She does not yet know how long ago, or from what, he died. But she does think it makes sense that Faye was a doctor's wife. She has the well-preserved look of a woman with the twin luxuries of money and time. Tamsin has seen, nesting in Faye's wardrobe, in the compartments of a complex timber grid, a large (but not obscenely large) number of shoes. Their soles are only lightly scratched, and the silks, satins, leathers and suedes of their uppers are creased only as much as would indicate careful wear. The same might be said of Faye's complexion.

Tamsin is chastened by Faye's personal habits. It is rare for her to drink anything other than water with a squeeze of lemon juice. She eats delicately, too: small plates of fig and passionfruit drizzled with just a little honey and plain yoghurt, undressed salads of rocket, pecan and pear. She tells Tamsin that she never cooks; she only buys fresh food that will look pleasing on a plate. This is what she tells Tamsin, and then she reminds herself, with a giggle, that she must consign this sentence to the past tense.

Each night Tamsin sleeps next to Michael in a bed beneath which is a suitcase. Because Michael has no curiosity, Tamsin has no need to lock it, even though it now contains things that she does not want him to see. On nights when he studies late at the library, she unpacks its contents onto the bed. She lays out the small white singlets, the small white hats, mittens and socks. And then she puts them away again.

Most nights Michael gets into bed beside her and kisses her, with intent.

And she kisses him back, without. And he takes up his book from the bedside table without asking why, or why not. She wishes that he would ask, because she has the answer ready. It is right there, just behind her bottom teeth, where she could oh-so-easily flick it up and onto her tongue. It's tainted, she would say, if only he would ask. Tarnished. She would give him words to conjure the metallic sheen of her spilled blood under bright lights.

4.

'Where is Kate?'

As time passes, this is the question Tamsin begins to carry with her up and down the aisles of supermarkets, stir into her pasta sauce, and squeeze onto her toothbrush late at night. It is the question that flares on the day that Faye's femur crumbles like plaster of Paris beneath the weight of her pelvis, the very last day of her life that she is able to stand on her feet. It steadily burns as weeks pass and Tamsin measures Faye's decline against the black-lined fractions of the syringes she draws up and plunges into needle-bruised skin. It will not be long now. And the telephone does not ring.

'You don't have any photos on display,' Tamsin observes one day.

'I like my pictures to be made of paint.'

'You must at least have some pictures of Kate.'

'I brought her into the world. Her face is the one I am least in danger of forgetting.'

It is one of the worst things for Tamsin: that the face she never saw is unrecoverable. Resentment snakes through her, a drug in her veins. It is general, indiscriminate. Kate may have been the only one ever to have curled up inside Faye's body, but she, Tamsin, will be the one to share the final intimacies of her life. She will give the needles that dull the pain, place the pillows that cushion the hollows of her body, wipe the shit from her shrivelled arse. She will be the true daughter at the end.

5.

'Where is Kate?' is the question Tamsin wants to ask Faye. She asks Michael instead, and his answers turn into a game.

'Perhaps she's a suburban drunk with nine grotty kids and she smokes the fag butts in the ashtrays at shopping centres.'

'Perhaps she's taken a vow of silence in a Mongolian yurt.'

'Perhaps she lives in a trailer park in Texas with a Mormon polygamist and his six other wives.'

'Perhaps she's not Kate anymore, but Kevin.'

Then one night he says:

'Perhaps it's not Kate that's the dark horse. Perhaps it's Faye. Maybe she murdered Kate and buried her beneath the hydrangeas.'

His stupidity wakes every sleeping thing inside of her and in an instant Tamsin can hear the thrumming and drumming of a thousand demons' tiny veined wings in her chest. Within three moves the conversation is a fight and soon he is saying it again:

'It wasn't the right time, love. We talked about this. My degree. Financially, we ...'

And she is getting shriller as she moves through her lines:

'Financially we killed our child so we could afford a nice house for our child to live in. We killed our baby so one day we could send it to a private school, so it could wear nice clothes. How does any of this make sense to you?'

He doesn't pull the punchline:

'Tam, it was a decision we made together.'

And she hates him, hates him, for saying it. Most of all because it is true. She hates him all the way up the stairs to the bedroom, and for all of the time it takes to take off her clothes and get into the shower. She wants to wash from her mind the orange-bricked building and its lay-back chair and its plug-hole swirling with her own red cells. Standing in the hot fall she feels an invisible cat kneading at her abdomen. Since the termination her periods have been clotty and painful. Now blood begins to fall from between her legs in heavy splotches. It is claret, then pink, as the diluting water swirls it towards the plughole.

After a while Michael opens the shower door, his look concerned, gentle. It makes her want to stretch her wet arms around him and pull him, clothes and all, into the shower with her. She wishes the droplets were her tears, and that he would stand in them until he was drenched. Then she sees him see the blood and she sees him think a thought he is too well-schooled to say out loud. But he doesn't have to say it. The damage is done. In place of concern there is relief – two-fold. His mouth tightens into a tiny patronising smile, and she wishes her hands were of the type that could flick out a set of long, sharp claws with which to scratch his face. She slams the shower door, catching his fingers, and when she sees through the beaded glass how he clutches them in pain, she is glad.

6.

'Where is Kate?' Tamsin finally asks Faye, on a day when her bitterness is so strong that she cannot help but make everyone else taste it too.

She asks her question with a careful measure of spite, her eyes on the face of her fob watch and her fingertips pressed firmly into the old woman's wrist. She expects to feel the pulse leap in concert with her own. But it does not.

'She's in the liquor cabinet.'

Tamsin flushes, hot with guilt. She has been cruel. And not only that, she has been cruel to an old woman whose mind – her sharp and beautiful mind – is following her body into decay. Tamsin has nursed more than one person through and beyond this point, but she had not thought that it would happen to Faye.

'In the liquor cabinet? I see.'

'That mollifying tone does not become you, you know.'

Tamsin looks away from the watch-face, losing count, to find Faye's eyes as clear as ever.

'And that crazy old biddy one doesn't do much for you either. You frightened me.'

'The anger goes, darling. I can promise you that much. It is the most volatile part, and it soon burns itself off.'

Tamsin flinches as if slapped. She had not known it could be seen from the outside.

'And then,' says Faye, 'there is only the sadness.'

7.

'Kate,' says Faye, 'really is in the liquor cabinet, you know.'

And on this day, which feels like one of the very last they will spend together, Tamsin is almost ready to believe her.

'You can take her out if you want to. I haven't taken her out for years.'

'So you have got a photo of her?'

'Go on. At the back.'

'Why wouldn't you show me before?'

'Behind the port.'

The ownership of a liquor cabinet is, to Tamsin – whose meagre supply of cheap booze sits in the corner of her kitchen cupboard – an index of elegance. A woman who owns a liquor cabinet is surely one who can coil her hair into a chignon and tong out lemon wedges with a demeanour as cool as the ice in her silver bucket. Tamsin imagines a young Faye, shaped like a *Vogue* paper pattern sketch, handing out drinks at a party.

The cabinet's rosewood doors open in her hands like those of an expensive car, smooth and substantial. Inside is the cut crystal of several decanters fitted with orbed stoppers. There is ruby port, sapphire gin, and something poisonously emerald. Tamsin removes the stopper and puts her nose to the neck.

'Crème de menthe? Yuck. Honestly Faye. And here I was thinking you had perfect taste.'

'At the back, at the back.'

And at the back, behind the port, Tamsin sees Kate.

Kate is small. Much smaller than Tamsin would have expected. Hers is a thick, glass jar with the word Fowlers pressed into the metal of its lid. Inside she floats, her delicate infant skin faintly rippled by the liquid preservative. Away from her belly twists a length of purplish flex, an umbilical cord to nowhere.

'Oh Faye.'

'Born too early, you see. Much too early. There was nothing that could be done.'

Tamsin touches a fingertip to the glass, as if she might trace the sculpted curves of the baby's tiny lips, or the sparse pale hairs of her eyebrows.

'I'd wanted her so much, I couldn't bear to leave the hospital without her. Keith arranged it for me, knew who to speak to. When I brought her home, I didn't know where to put her. The liquor cabinet seemed somehow … ironic. When happiness is no longer possible, you see, one might as well try to keep oneself amused.'

Tamsin is gentle, but when she lifts the jar she cannot prevent the foetus from bobbing stiffly in her formalin bath, knees and elbows fending glass.

'Let me see her.'

Tamsin cradles Kate in her arms for a moment before handing her to her mother, propped on the pillows of her bed.

Faye takes her tenderly and when her tears fall, they touch glass, dissolving into its thickness.

8.

'Kate,' Tamsin thinks.

It is the first thing she thinks on the day she arrives to find the apartment's front door, its windows and the rear of an ambulance left gapingly, indecently, open. It is as if it is Faye's corpse so carelessly exposed. Tamsin ditches her bike on the street and rushes, wanting desperately to draw a nightgown down over the whole, horrible scene.

The night nurse is on the patio, smoking and looking out over the river, her long ribbed cardigan tightly twisted around her torso. Faye's nephew is there too, but he cannot settle to sitting or standing or leaning. His movements criss-cross the near-white carpet but avoid the men in blue coveralls who have clipboards and kind faces. They have already moved Faye out of her own bed and onto the hard and narrow mattress of the ambulance trolley.

Tamsin touches the now slightly yellowed skin of her face, smoothes the soft lilac of her hair. The nephew watches as if Tamsin were television.

'She liked you.'

'I liked her.'

'Thank you. For making her comfortable.'

Tamsin lifts Faye's bird-bone hand and touches the back of it to her cheek. She lays it down again and nods to the ambulance officer who clicks off the brakes and begins to wheel the trolley towards the door.

'She wanted you to have something,' the nephew tells Tamsin. 'She said you could choose.'

Tamsin wonders if he knows how obviously his eyes flicker to the smallest of the paintings, the ones he is not sure she knows are the most valuable of all. So easily could she claim one, just a small one, and all in the guise of being too modest to pick a larger canvas.

'Anything. She did say anything.'

Tamsin sees how he must fight himself to say this, and by what a narrow margin his better self wins.

'Could I have one of the decanters? From the liquor cabinet.'

'A decanter? Good god, you can have the lot.'

9.

'Kate,' Tamsin answers the woman making expert tucks in tissue paper on the counter.

'Short for Katherine?'

'No. Just Kate.'

'How nice to hear a nice plain name. Almost unusual nowadays, isn't it? And how old?'

'Twelve ... yes, twelve months.'

'Oh you do have to think, don't you? Goes so quickly. Before you know it, they're asking for the car keys.'

Twelve months. Can it really have been so long? Tamsin has not the usual milestones – sitting, crawling, standing, walking – to help her keep track.

'Twelve months,' the woman says, clucking her tongue. 'Oh they're lovely at that age, aren't they? Well, I'm sure your little Kate will look adorable in these.'

They are shoes, this time, of the softest pink leather. Tamsin checks her watch. Now that Michael is working again, there is no need to rush. There is plenty of time yet, before he gets home, to add to her accumulation of secrets in the suitcase beneath the bed. In the street she sits at an outdoor café table and watches the movements of doctors' wives and flowers and glossy cars. Into the boutique from which she has just come, go women with loose shirts over growing bellies. But Tamsin does not envy them. Not any more.

Aunt Matilda's Party Dress

Jena Woodhouse

It was one of those increasingly rare occasions for us, a family gathering. Not the whole clan, which is pretty humungous. It was spur-of-the-moment. My mum, my brothers and I decided to go and wish Mum's sister, Nance, a happy birthday. We didn't have any money for a present, but we've gotten used to not having money for stuff like that since Dad's been gone, so Mum simply got down to it and did her usual birthday thing: made a cake and some Anzac biscuits, and off we went.

We'd just demolished the cake, all gathered round in the kitchen with Aunty Nance's husband and kids, when we heard somebody yoo-hooing through the living room, and who should appear in our midst but Aunt Mat.

Aunt Mat is something of a legend in our family. She travels a lot, so what we hear of her is often secondhand. She has a slightly mysterious, rather glamorous image, and I've heard her referred to as a dark horse, a black sheep, a lame duck, an enfant terrible, a bohemian, and a bit of a nomad. Depending on who is telling the story. My mum's very religious, although she's pretty understanding too, mostly. Matilda, as far as we know, has no fixed religion.

Anyway, the odd thing is, when you meet Matilda, she seems neither glamorous nor mysterious. She always looks as if her clothes were thrown together without much thought. On this occasion she was wearing a warm black top under a fluffy, sleeveless vest, but the other half of her outfit didn't match at all. The bottom half consisted of daggy old tracksuit pants, and then, although it was winter, open sandals. Red hair (like mine), pale face, no make-up. That's my Aunt Mat.

She'd brought various bundles to distribute, another thing she's famous for. Birthday presents for Nance: two fluffy sleeveless vests like the one she was wearing herself, still with the price-tags on. Various hand-me-downs, not very interesting. Mat's weight fluctuates, so she's always offloading things that are suddenly either too big or too small. But nobody ever looked good in her cast-offs. You needed her kind of personality to get away with the outfits she wore, which were an original mixture of daggy and daring. (Half poodle, half blue heeler, Uncle Ted once rudely said.) So I wasn't taking much notice, until she pulled out a scrunched-up black thing, gleaming here and there where it caught the light.

She gave it a shake and held it up, and it fell into the shape of a dress, a little black party dress, very plain, except for the beading on the bodice, shiny jet beads sewn in a pattern to form a deep V, accentuating the narrow, plunging neckline.

As soon as I saw it, I wanted it. That dress was made for me. I hoped Aunt Nance wouldn't put in a bid, seeing it was her birthday. But Aunt Mat was looking at me as if something had just occurred to her.

'Here, Janey,' she was saying. 'I brought it for Nance, but you could wear this. I picked it up in Paris, years ago, when I was young and slim.'

Out of the corner of my eye, I saw Mum open her mouth as if to say something, then think better of it, and snap her lips shut like a coin purse. Everyone was looking at me. I was looking at Mat. Did she really mean it? She was holding the dress out for me to take. I looked at Mum for permission, but she gave no sign, just kept her lips tightly compressed. Nance didn't seem to want it either. She was into a more sporty look, you never saw her in slinky outfits.

I stretched out my fingers and touched the silky fabric. It

felt almost alive. Mat sort of thrust it into my hand. They were all still watching, and then Nance said: 'Aren't you going to try it on?'

I shook my head.

Someone found a carry bag and the dress was bundled away out of sight, as if it was something scandalous or provocative. Then Nance and Mum made cups of tea and we took them out onto the deck.

Aunt Mat sidled up to me. 'I hope you enjoy the dress,' she said. 'It's been to many magical evenings: operas, parties, embassies, glamorous nights along the Seine, in Montparnasse. I'm glad it's yours now, Janey. Hope it brings you happiness. I always used to wear it to attract good luck.'

My head was on fire. Good luck in what, I wondered. True love? Success and fame? Mat had been unfortunate in both respects, they said. She wasn't exactly wealthy, either, and her career in art (she was a sculptor) had more downs than ups.

Very quietly I said, 'If Mum lets me wear it.'

Just at that moment, Mum, sniffing conspiracy, moved closer. 'You really shouldn't be giving Janey clothes that are far too old for her,' she reproached Mat.

Mat was diplomatic. 'It's such an elegant little number, Gracey, don't you think? And young beauties like Janey, with her artist's model hair, look stunning in simple black, trust me! It's the last word in chic and *savoir-vivre*! You can't keep her rigged out like the von Trapps for much longer. After all, she's turning seventeen this year, isn't she?'

Well, I doubted the dress would be going anywhere, at least on me. But fortunately Nance stepped in and changed the subject.

When we got home, I locked myself in my room, saying I had an important French assignment due on Monday. This was true. But first of all, I took off all my clothes and slithered into the new satin camisole and knickers Nance had given me. I slipped the elastic band off my ponytail, and took a long look at myself in the mirror. To my surprise, I liked what I saw – my smooth, creamy-white neck and shoulders, the satin clinging to my breasts, reminded me of one of Aunt Mat's little clay maquettes of nymphs and dancers.

Then I took the dress out of the plastic bag, taking care not to make any loud rustling sounds, and slowly, very gently, lowered it over my head.

It was a perfect fit. I closed my eyes, then opened them again. There was a hint of old, expensive perfume coming from the silk, and a faint but not unpleasant whiff of smoke. I fancied I could also smell the musky scent of skin, of flesh, but it was so subtle, maybe I was imagining it. I closed my eyes again, and I had the weird sensation of drinking in another world through the pores of my skin, a feeling as though someone's arms were enveloping me. I could feel my body moving in harmony with the other, the stranger's, a slow dance in a smoky room whose windows overlooked the Seine. I even fancied I could hear the murmur of voices, speaking French. I slowly circled in my room, dancing with eyes closed, synchronising my breathing with my imaginary partner's.

So at first I didn't hear Mum tapping at my door, not until she thumped it more insistently. 'Jane!' she shouted, 'Open up at once!'

Panicking, I twisted the key, grabbed the door handle and wrenched the door open so suddenly that she almost fell into the room. Bracing herself, she glared at me in frigid disapproval. Of course, the dress. I'd been so startled by her sudden knocking that I'd forgotten.

'What do you think this is?' she began indignantly. Then, in a quieter, more ominous tone, 'Take it off at once! I don't know what Matilda's thinking of, giving an innocent young girl clothes you'd see in a French film that no respectable person would watch! Look at the way it exposes your chest! It's indecent, not to mention unhealthy! What would the pastor say?'

'Don't look at me then!' was all I could reply.

As soon as she turned her back, I pulled off the dress and put on my ordinary clothes.

She turned and snatched the little black dress, its beading

flashing and glinting defiantly. 'I'll take that,' she said. 'I'll put it away where it won't give you the wrong kinds of ideas.'

I knew it would be useless to protest. Perhaps I'd never see the tantalising garment again. She'd bundle it into the bag of old clothes to donate to Lifeline. But what she didn't know was that now, having seen myself in that dress, and danced the slow, erotic dance in a room above the Seine, nothing could ever be quite the same. In those few minutes that I had worn it, the dress had become my dream passport. I didn't yet know where I'd be getting off the plane, but it would be there, in my luggage, one day ...

Notes on Contributors

Alli Barnard is eighteen years old and had her first short story published in *Best Australian Stories 2004*. She was a prize-winner in the *Sydney Morning Herald*–Sydney Theatre Company young playwrights competition last year. This story was accepted by the private magazine *Aurora* published by the Renzo Piano building trust, Sydney. She is currently studying Fine Arts at the University of Sydney.

Nathan Besser is a young writer from Sydney. Since his first publication in *Best Australian Stories 2004* he has had another story accepted by the *Griffith Review* (November 2005).

David Campbell is a Melbourne writer and mathematician whose stories and poetry have won a number of recent awards. In late 2004 he and his wife co-authored *Simply Poetry!* an illustrated book of original poems for pre-school children published by Tertiary Press. 'The Other Place' first appeared in *Meanjin*.

Patrick Cullen's writing has been recognised in a number of regional and national awards including the 2003 and 2004 *Age* Short Story Awards, and the 2005 Alan Marshall Short Story Award. 'And?', 'Mauve' and 'Collapsing Under Their Own Weight' are part of a collection of five stories submitted for a BA (Hons.) at the University of Newcastle. He is currently completing a Master of Creative Arts at the University of Newcastle. His story 'And?' has been accepted for publication in the next edition of *The Sleepers Almanac.*

Peter Goldsworthy's most recent book was *The List of All Answers: Collected Stories,* published by Penguin Viking. A stage adaptation of his 1991 novel *Honk If You Are Jesus* will premiere at the 2006 Adelaide Festival.

Melissa Goode was born in Sydney and has studied history and law. She currently lives in Melbourne. 'The Only Damage' was a runner-up in the Josephine Ulrick national short story competition. It is her first published story.

Janette Turner Hospital received the Patrick White Award for lifetime literary achievement in 2003. Her most recent novel is *Due Preparations for the Plague.* 'Blind Date' first appeared in *The Monthly.*

Graeme Kinross-Smith is a poet, writer of fiction and photographer working in Melbourne, Geelong and Port Campbell. His novel *Long Afternoon of the World* (Wakefield Press) will be published in 2006.

Joanna Kujawa has published stories and non-fiction in Australia, Canada, the UK and Poland. She is currently working on a novel exploring sexual desire and mysticism in different religious traditions.

Chris Mansell is primarily a poet who has published half a dozen books and other material. She has also had a number of plays performed and writes short fiction from time to time. She's won a few things, and been short-listed for others. Her most recent book *Mortifications & Lies* was published by Kardoorair Press in 2005. Her site is at: www.chris.mansell.name.

Karen Manton lives and works in Batchelor, Northern Territory. Her work was published in the NT Literary Awards 2003 anthology and *True North: Contemporary Writing of the Northern Territory* (2004), and she is the author of *The gift of Julian of Norwich* (2005). Awards include the Arafura Short Story Award (2003) and the NT Fistful of Films best screenplay awards (2002, 2004). She was the 2004 recipient of Varuna's Eleanor Dark Fellowship (best project in fiction) for her novel in progress, *The glass spinner*. Her favourite pastime is walking along a beach or through the bush with her dog Tojo.

Alejandra Martinez lives in the Blue Mountains of NSW with her partner and three children. She was born in Uruguay and came to Australia when she was seven years old. She was published in *Best Australian Stories 2004*.

Gillian Mears' last collection of stories *A Map of the Gardens* was awarded the Steele Rudd prize in 2003.

Paul Mitchell's fiction has appeared in *Overland* and *Island* magazines, as well as Cardigan Press (2003) and *The Sleepers Almanac* (2005). His poetry book *Minorphysics* (Interactive Publications, 2003) won the 2003 IP Picks Award for best unpublished Australian manuscript.

Amra Pajalic lives in Sydney with her husband and two cats and is currently working on a young adult novel.

Alison Ravenscroft won the Josephine Ulrick national short story prize with 'Object Lessons' in 2005. She teaches Australian and American literature in the English Department at La Trobe University, Melbourne. 'Object Lessons' was published in the November 2005 issue of the *Griffith Review*.

Sue Robertson is a Melbourne writer whose love of writing was fostered and continues to be nurtured by a group spawned by the Centre for Adult Education, now known as the Tuesday

Writers. She has had stories published in the weekly and popular magazines as well as anthologies. She was runner-up in the *Herald Sun* Competition in 2003 and has been highly commended in a number of other competitions. She has just completed her first novel.

Janey Runci has had short stories published in *Meanjin, Fine Line, Australasian Post* and an anthology, *Red Hot Notes.* In 2004 she was runner-up in the Bridport Prize in the UK and runner-up in the Boroondara Competition. This story was written at a Freefall writing workshop with the Canadian teacher–writer, Barbara Turner-Vesselago. Janey lives in Maldon, Victoria.

Girija Tropp's work has appeared in *Agni 61, The Boston Review* and a Visible Ink anthology and online at elimae, Opium, Zoetrope All-Story Extra, Word Riot and Margin, forthcoming at Pineldyboz.

Tara June Winch was born near Sydney in 1983, where she spent her childhood roaming the shorelines of the NSW south-coast, swimming and surfing. Tara is of Wiradjuri, Afghan and English heritage. In 2004 she won the National David Unaipon Award for her novella *Swallow the Air* which will be published by University of Queensland Press this year. 'Cloud Busting' is an extract.

Charlotte Wood's last novel *The Submerged Cathedral* was shortlisted for the 2005 Miles Franklin Award and the Commonwealth Writers' Prize, South East Asia/South Pacific. Her first novel *Pieces of a Girl* earned her a commendation among the *Sydney Morning Herald* Best Young Novelists in 2000. She lives in Sydney with her husband Sean, and is writing a third novel.

Danielle Wood won the 2002 *The Australian*/Vogel Literary Prize and the 2004 Dobbie Award for her first novel *The Alphabet of Light and Dark.* She teaches writing at the University of Tasmania and is working on two projects: a second novel and a collection of contemporary fairy tales for grown-up girls. 'The True Daughter' first appeared in *The Monthly*.

Jena Woodhouse's publications include two poetry collections, *Eros in Landscape* (1989) and *Passenger on a Ferry* (1994), and an award-winning novella for children, *Metis, the Octopus and the Olive Tree* (1994). A degree in Russian literary studies fuelled a passion for writing, and she is currently working on a Ph.D in Creative Writing at Queensland University of Technology.